GOD'S FIRE
ON ICE

GOD'S FIRE ON ICE

Kayy Gordon with Lois Neely

LOGOS INTERNATIONAL
Plainfield, New Jersey

GOD'S FIRE ON ICE
Copyright © 1977 by Logos International
All Rights Reserved
Printed in the United States of America
International Standard Book Number: 0-88270-249-1
Library of Congress Catalog Card Number: 77-90825
Logos International, Plainfield, New Jersey 07061

919.8
G

Table of Contents

Introduction vii

The Call
1   The Arctic Storm. 3
2   A Time to Learn 9
3   Alone with a Vision 17
4   Anna and Mikkel 23

Into the North
5   My Promised Land 31
6   Winter in a Tent 61
7   The Dark Winter Night 69
8   Spirit-Filled Eskimos 73
9   Journey by Dog Team 79

Pioneering with the Gospel
10   Tuk 87
11   The Church on the Tundra 95
12   The Reindeer Camp 101
13   Iona 109
14   Outreach to Alaska 115
15   Springtime in the Arctic 121

33306

Cambridge Bay—Reaching Out

16 The Settlement   129
17 Igloo *Pinektok*   137
18 God Breaks Through   143
19 The Flesh Is Weak   149
20 An Eskimo Apostle Paul   159
21 Arctic Ways of Life and Death   163
22 Ruth and Nels   171
23 Iona's Vision   177
24 Alcohol—a Major Problem   189
25 Youth Work and Community Involvement   197
26 Powers of the *Anagkok*   209

And to the Uttermost

27 Bible School   217
28 God Doesn't Forget   229
29 More Opportunities   237
30 Treasures of the Snow   249

Epilogue   253

Introduction

In late August, 1972, I was in the high Arctic on a writing assignment for a travel magazine. My float plane sank in gale winds, leaving me stranded in the remote Eskimo settlement of Cambridge Bay, 200 miles north of the Arctic Circle. I was penniless and totally alone, but not for long. I walked along that bleak Arctic Ocean shore, the snow stinging my face, praying, "My God, are you really with me in this desolate place?"

He was, for He guided me to a little mission with an apartment above, and I knocked on the side door. (Kayy told me later she knew it was a white person, because no native would knock.) "Please, may I come in? I'm so cold and so tired." And secretly to God I added, "Please do a little extra to prove your love for me and to renew my faith in the family of God. Please let them offer me something to eat." I hadn't eaten for the past eighteen hours.

Although I was a total stranger, they welcomed me with a warm hug. No sooner were my parka and boots off than a mug of steaming coffee was beside me. "How about a grilled cheese sandwich, Lois?" My heart fairly burst with praise and thanksgiving, and a sense of belonging to God's great family. But still I had not revealed to them that I too was a child of our wonderful, all-caring Father.

We chatted over lunch. They asked no questions. Gradually I told them who I was: a housewife and mother, an administrator of our church's home for seniors near Toronto, Canada. But the love of my life was writing. I wrote mostly for *Reader's Digest*. Other writing included travel articles and some work for Billy Graham's *Decision* magazine where I helped in their Schools of Writing.

But what were these two sparkling, fun-loving girls doing stuck away in this remote, godless Eskimo settlement? Marian Page was a nurse (probably in her early thirties, I figured) often called upon hurriedly for mercy flights south, perhaps to help an Eskimo woman brutally stabbed in a drunken brawl. But mostly, she was called of God to help Kayy.

Kayy Gordon—a vivacious, blue-eyed blonde, somewhere in

her thirties too—a slight, five-foot bundle of effortless "can-do" energy. Her pace was relaxed enough to fit the native way of life; yet her achievements were incredible. The very existence of this fine building was proof, with its warm, spacious sanctuary down below, and a comfortable apartment above. It has a kitchen to be envied by any housewife, complete with a dishwasher, and a living room with a four-by-eight-foot picture window looking over the bay. ("You can't possibly get a piece of glass that big into the Arctic, Kayy," the men had told her.) Also, there was a modern three-piece bathroom with hot and cold running water, and nicely furnished bedrooms. (What a treat it was to be tucked between flowered, perma-press sheets after days on the tundra!)

After a time of rest and recuperation, I attended a service which was led by the Eskimos. Afterward, I sat on the floor of the living room, drinking tea with giggling Eskimo young people who showed me some of their native tricks and games and wrestled for me.

Later, I went with Kayy to the post office. Kayy Gordon had been postmistress of Cambridge Bay for twelve years. Like Paul of old, she supported herself and contributed to the ministry. She showed me the first house she had built for herself in Cambridge Bay. She also told me of her first twelve months in the Arctic. During that first year, she lived in a tent with the reindeer herders. She told me of her 400-mile treks by dog sled and snowmobile to minister to the caribou hunters. (Not until later when I stood on the shores of Hudson Bay and saw the crazy tangles and heaves of ice blocks and ridges, did I fully appreciate how difficult such a journey would be.) I saw her counseling, mediating, and encouraging the Christians and the drunks. And I knew that the natives obviously loved her.

She shared with me her vision of an Eskimo church that would be Bible-taught and totally self-sufficient, ministering to its own people across the desolate wastes of three quarters of a million square miles of ice, snow and unmarked tundra.

After only three days I had to leave. As Kayy stood on the float dock waving to me in the Twin Otter, I realized that I had met one of God's chosen servants, a truly remarkable young woman.

I have been back north several times and talked with Eskimos and whites. Always, I have found that Kayy Gordon is one of the most respected white women of the Canadian Arctic.

One day Kayy called me from Vancouver and said, "Lois, let's write a book." I was staggered, but overjoyed. As we met in Toronto and I had the pleasure of returning her hospitality, I found that Kayy was equally at home in our best restaurants as when she was sitting on caribou skins eating raw seal meat and drinking tea from a mug that was rubbed clean by a rag that had just wiped a runny nose.

Kayy and I wrote this story together. It is a story of God's provision, of His faithfulness and great goodness—this procession of miracles across a land that is incredibly forbidding with temperatures often hovering at 85 below, with hardships that defy description. It is an account of God's grace being extended to these gentle, dignified, gracious Inuit, a people of limitless patience and hospitality, who seem to be equal to any emergency, and who have taken to their hearts this tiny white woman—*Eyikpak*, or "Big Eyes"—and have embraced her and her God.

Lois Neely

The Call

CHAPTER 1

The Arctic Storm

It was a frigid 65 below in January as we pushed our way across the barren lands of the Canadian Arctic. Two hours earlier a cloud of fog and snow had settled over the trail, shutting us off from our guide. We stumbled on. The dogs were hungry, tired and upset. They pulled first in this direction, then that, and were fighting and restless.

Finally, I stopped. As I stood on the back of the toboggan with the snow swirling blindingly about us and the dogs snapping, snarling, tangling their harness, a feeling of helpless frustration came over me.

"Iona, let's face it. We're completely lost," I heard myself say. "The wind has whipped away all traces of the lead team's tracks, and in this fog and darkness, I don't know how we can find our way."

"But, oh, God," I prayed silently, "please, somehow, make a way for us. I've brought this unsaved nurse with me and I don't want to be an instrument of her death."

Iona sat on the toboggan, staring grimly into the storm. Four days earlier, we had started out from the little Eskimo community of Tuktoyaktuk, high up along the bleak shores of the Arctic Ocean, just east of the Mackenzie River Delta. It had taken seventeen hours of hard traveling over the soft snow with our dog team to reach the reindeer herders' camp. There Iona, a government nurse, checked the babies and gave them their inoculations, and I preached. We stayed two days and then with Nels, our Lapland guide, we headed back to Tuk. Winds came up, whirling the snow in clouds that blocked out the landscape. What little daylight there is in January had slipped away, so we decided to camp in an abandoned igloo and wait for the moon to come up.

The going was so slow that we ran out of gasoline for our primus stove (a two-burner camp stove); all our food was frozen, so we couldn't eat. We couldn't thaw the snow for a cup of tea. Spreading our reindeer skins on the snow and climbing into our sleeping bags with our parkas and boots on, I remember thinking that I would never be warm again. Outside the hungry dogs howled, and the wind swirled and moaned around the igloo.

At moonrise we rose and struggled to hitch up the two teams. Nels was ready first and took off, because once the dogs are hitched you have to go. This was only my second year with a dog team and I was having a difficult time. I was always reluctant to whip them, but finally they were hitched and we started off. As we came over the ridge, I realized with dismay that the fog had dropped and I could no longer see Nels. We followed his tracks a little way, until all traces of them had been wiped out by the gusting winds.

Which way should we go? A compass is no use in the far north, and the dogs seemed confused. I'd try to get them going one way, but they kept changing directions. Finally, I stopped, prayed a simple prayer and then said, "Iona, I'm going to let the dogs proceed." I knew that I couldn't direct them, so I prayed that God would.

For a few minutes the dogs floundered around. Then they took off in a different direction altogether, purposefully now and pointing straight. There was no more tangling or fighting. For about an hour we traveled in the darkness and fog. Only a little moonlight filtered through. Suddenly the dogs speeded up. About ten minutes later, just as suddenly, the blowing snow cleared momentarily. In that moment I caught a fleeting glimpse of dark figures moving against the shimmering snow about a quarter of a mile away. It had to be Nels! Just as quickly, the swirling snow again shut off the view. I turned the team and they responded. In just a few minutes we had caught up.

"Praise the Lord!" Nels shouted as we came within earshot. His voice was vibrant with gratitude and joy. He had been gravely concerned about us, knowing that we were obviously lost and had no food or shelter. "Oh, God, guide them," Nels had prayed. His inclination had been to turn around immediately and begin to search for us, but somehow he had hesitated. Had he turned and begun that search, our trails might never have met, and Iona and I would have been lost permanently. Oh, the goodness of God!

It's easy to be lost in the Arctic during any season. It's not unusual to roam in summer over the hills and become completely turned around, because even in broad daylight, the land looks so much the same. Years later, when I could be considered a seasoned northerner, I've been known to be lost only a few miles from the village. In any season, the joy of being found is always indescribable, but to be lost in the killing cold of winter, and then to be found, is an ecstasy of joy.

Once our team had caught up to Nels, the night was still cold, the wind was still blowing, and the visibility still very limited, but somehow I didn't notice the bite of the wind. Now I could relax, content just to see that dog team ahead of us.

Before long we sighted the DEW line beacon at Tuk, a red saucer of light against the dark, arctic night and a welcome landmark for all travelers in the north. Even the dogs seemed to gain their second wind. They knew that home was just an hour or so away.

At last the lights of the village dotted the darkness, and we could almost feel the warmth of those snug houses and the glow of hot tea and friendly faces. As the lights grew brighter, the dogs quickened their pace. Soon we heard the familiar howl of all the other dogs in the village announcing our arrival.

Some of the men nearby came to unharness the dogs and chain them to their stakes. With great delight I pulled off my outer parka and fur pants, and stumbled into my little, green plywood shack that somehow seemed like a mansion. Quickly, the Christian Eskimos began to come in. Very soon reindeer soup was heated up, and hot tea—so welcome to our stiff cold bodies. The warmth of their love and care for us, the joy of being with them again, suddenly made the rigors of the trip very worthwhile.

Coming in from the arctic storm that had almost entrapped us, I had a special appreciation for my house. The little old oil heater was throwing out its great heat; even sitting on a bench instead of squatting on a tent floor was satisfying. I had such a feeling of security in that little home. Its walls were strong. Winter winds could not penetrate them. As I finally laid down that night on my bunk, with reindeer skins for my mattress and a sleeping bag for my blanket, I dropped off into a sound sleep thanking God for His goodness.

Several hours later I woke up. Lying on the reindeer skin, I looked around at the bare wood walls, the single gas lantern dangling from the ceiling, the oil space heater that doubled as an altar, the tiny primus stove perched on an orange crate and my one luxury—a wooden sleeping platform—tucked in a corner. Sparsely furnished? Not when jammed wall-to-wall each night with hungry-hearted Eskimos.

Outside, the wind still whistled and howled. The sun would peek over the horizon for about an hour, then twilight and darkness would fall again. Could it only be twenty months since I left

Vancouver? Balmy Vancouver—a city of skyscrapers and charming homes set against the magnificent backdrop of towering, snow-capped mountains rising out of the blue Pacific; a shoreline with deep fjords slicing into the black and green of rock and forest. Only twenty months—yet surely light-years away.

Had my church encouraged me to come north? Hardly. "Crazy Kayy!" they chided. My dream of the Arctic had been the joke of the congregation. My family, my Christian co-workers, my pastor—all had discouraged me. "Why can't you feel called to somewhere nice and conventional like Africa or Taiwan?" they'd ask. "Nobody goes as a missionary to the Arctic." They'd shake their heads incredulously as my notion only grew stronger.

Finally I went north in June of 1956, a starry-eyed, twenty-two-year-old visionary who was determined to light a fire for God in the frozen wastes of the Canadian Arctic. I had so much to teach the Eskimos.

But how much they had taught me—of true kindness, of generosity of spirit, of plain, simple gratitude, of caring for their brother, of courage in desperate situations. I had fished and hunted with them, feasting on caribou heads and ptarmigan stew. For fourteen months I had lived in a double canvas tent among the reindeer herders, through a winter when 45 below was the norm. And then, under the midnight sun, with the help of a dear Eskimo girl, I had built this shack on the windswept shores of the Arctic Ocean.

Yes, I had walked in their *mukluks* (sealskin overboots), slept in their igloos, and now the Holy Spirit was beginning to move in this desolate and lonely, but not God-forsaken, settlement of the high Arctic.

Vancouver? It seemed to be on another planet.

CHAPTER 2

A Time to Learn

"God knows your address and phone number, Kayy. When He wants you, He'll call you." With these words, my pastor gently reminded me. It was June, 1953, and I was an insistent, demanding teenager.

But was I ever impatient. Why couldn't Pastor Layzell understand that God was calling me to the Arctic? Had He not called me to the ministry even before I was born? Not until after I was saved and had renounced my burning ambition to be a lawyer, had mother told me of the vision she had seen almost as soon as she was aware that she had conceived me, her seventh child. Mother was a seeker after God, but not yet a true born-again believer. She had gone to the back yard and while lying on the grass, she lifted her heart to God.

"Oh, Lord," she prayed, "let this last child be a minister, but not the ordinary kind of minister. Let him be one who challenges people." As she opened her eyes, she looked up through the leaves of the trees and saw the form of a cross. From that moment on, mother firmly believed that God had heard and would answer her prayer. Then, when I was born—a girl!—mother's heart sank. God had not granted her request, she thought, for whoever heard of a woman minister?

As I grew up on the Canadian prairie, mother's doubts certainly appeared to be accurate. Stubborn and rebellious, with no interest in religion—that was the Kayy mother saw. With older brothers and sisters doting and waiting on me, I had no need to talk. Consequently, I was over two years old before I burst out with a sentence. I commanded, "Iris, get dat ball!" My family has never let me forget that my first words were in the imperative form.

Right from the start there was a determined, independent streak that would stand me in good stead in my arctic life. When I was three-and-a-half I became impatient waiting for my brothers to read the comics to me, so I announced that I was going to learn to read for myself. My older sister, Iris, became my accomplice. She would eavesdrop on the first grade lessons in the one-room school in northern Saskatchewan, then come home and teach me. Before the year was out I could write, add, subtract, and best of all, read those comics by myself! It was just at this time I announced I would be a lawyer, and that was that.

Father died quite suddenly, when I was only nine, after suffering many years with diabetes. The rest of the children were grown, and I was left with my mother who had been afflicted soon after my birth with crippling multiple sclerosis. She and I became very close as increasingly there was more that I had to do for her. I would shop for her, go to the bank, and pay the bills. These lessons would prove to be invaluable in the work God called me to do. At that time, however, I felt only rebellion against God. I would often find myself thinking, "Why do I have to be saddled with sick, old parents? Why couldn't I have had a young mother and father like the other kids?"

Mother and I moved from the farm to the city of Prince Albert. One day, as we entered the Princess Cafe on Central Avenue, a young man stepped in front of us. Noticing mother's crutches, he told us about a man of God, William Branham, who prayed for sick people. He explained that many were healed at his services. Mother's eyes lit up. We had traveled constantly from doctor to doctor searching for help with her dread multiple sclerosis.

"Shall we go to Calgary to hear this man, Kayy?" mother asked.

The idea didn't appeal to me at all. My father, the most generous of all men, was an agnostic. The goal he set before me in life was to get a good education, with good earning power. In Prince Albert, mother and I attended a Presbyterian church where I galloped through eight years of catechism in nine months, and memorized reams of Scripture. This wasn't because I was interested. I was simply highly competitive, with a drive to excel in everything I did.

By the time I was fourteen, I had decided my father was right—there wasn't anything of great value in religion. The more I learned, the more I was turned off. So I decided if I could get away from any church involvement without hurting my mother, I would do it. But now she was asking if I would go with her to the special healing meetings in Calgary. Although I wasn't happy about it, I agreed to go.

I'll never forget that evening—5,000 people who seemed to be actually enjoying their religion! Their singing especially fascinated me. It was joyful and alive, as if the people really knew and meant what they were singing about.

Then a little man stood up and in a very quiet, humble way told of God's call on his life and of the gift of healing the Lord had given him. We were seated at the front in the area set aside for wheelchairs. A little boy, whose eyes were badly crossed, was brought to the platform for prayer. With a heart obviously filled with love and tenderness, Brother Branham prayed a simple prayer of faith that must have shaken the sinners and saints alike. When the child turned again to face the congregation, his eyes were as straight as could be.

Even though my mother was not healed, the boy's miracle left a profound impression on this smart-aleck teenager. I had actually witnessed at close range the miraculous power of God. There was no denying it.

The next afternoon I was back again. The singing seemed even better, the whole place more vibrant with joy. When the evangelist preached, the words came through loud and clear. "Are you ready for eternity?" he thundered. I knew I wasn't ready. As the altar call was given, a tremendous struggle within began to tear me apart. They sang the first verse of "Just As I Am." Others were going forward, but I couldn't. They sang the second, the third, the fourth and fifth stanzas. How I wanted to walk down that aisle, but I was glued to my place!

Then they sang the sixth stanza and a strange thing happened. An aunt who was not living for the Lord, but happened to be in that meeting, tapped me on the shoulder. "Kayy, would you like to make things right? I'll go with you to the altar," she gently suggested. That was all I needed.

When I got to the altar I didn't know what to do; I didn't know how to pray. The workers instructed me to simply invite Christ into my life, to ask Him to forgive my sins. I did this, then got up from my knees, not aware of any great change or experience.

But the next morning when I woke up, there was a desire in my heart that had never been there before. Without hesitating, I went to my mother and asked, "Mom, do we have a Bible?" When she gave me grandma's old Bible, I grabbed it eagerly and began to read. For the first time, the Bible was more than just words. It had meaning to me and it possessed a message. I was flooded with a great joy, to think I could actually understand God's Word a little! Closing the Bible, I turned to my mother.

"Mom, do you know what I want to do when I finish school?" I asked.

She looked at me. "Kayy, from the time you were a little tot you said you wanted to be a lawyer.''

"No, mom," I answered, "I want to be a preacher."

And with that my mother burst into tears and told me the story of her prayer and vision before I was born. God *was* faithful. He was going to answer her prayers.

Mother too found Jesus Christ as her Savior during those meetings in Calgary, and together we were baptized in water the next week. We all had to testify, and afterwards several people said to mom, "That girl of yours is going to be a preacher one day."

God now put it into my mother's heart to make some wise decisions about our future. In Prince Albert, I had been accelerated two years in school, and because I was so much smaller and younger I had assumed the role of daredevil in order to be accepted by the older group. The opposite sex was becoming very attractive, and I was scheming how I could have a part in the exciting sexual escapades I'd heard the older kids talking about. Mother didn't think we should return to Prince Albert and one day she said, "Let's find a new home in a new city for our new life in Christ."

I came to sophisticated Vancouver as an awkward, self-conscious shrimp of a teenager, with a deep inferiority complex which had developed over the years. These feelings were caused mostly by my teeth—or lack of them.

When I was four, Dad decided that two loose front teeth should go. "One dollar for each tooth, Kayy," he said, fixing the pliers firmly on the first tooth. But those two teeth weren't so loose. I refused to cry, put the two dollars under my pillow and sobbed myself to sleep with the pain. For the next four years I remained toothless, and the kids teased and razzed me mercilessly. Finally, the second teeth came in, but to my dismay, they stuck out. Buck teeth! I'd spend hours twisting my jaw this way and that, trying to improve my appearance.

So when the Vancouver dentist discovered that I had several cavities, I said, "No fillings. Pull the whole works." He was horrified. But that upper plate changed my whole personality.

Now it was fun to meet new friends. No more twisting or hiding my misshapen teeth. It was as if a tent had been lifted from me, and an outgoing Kayy had emerged.

I dashed through the last three years of high school with more interest in Christian work than high grades. Now that I wasn't going into law, why struggle to win a scholarship? I know now that that was a mistake, an immature attitude.

I was headed straight for Bible school and the ministry. But Pastor Reg Layzell had other ideas. At Glad Tidings Temple, my mom and I had found a church home that suited us, a happy, joyful fellowship. Pastor Layzell became my father figure, a very strong man of God whom I deeply respected and loved. My brothers and sisters were shocked that I had abandoned my plans for law school. They may have resented the impact Pastor Layzell had on my life. My brother wryly remarked, "The gospel according to Kayy has at least three people in heaven: God on the throne, Jesus by His side, and Pastor Layzell next in command."

A disciplinarian of high standards, our pastor demanded much from his young people. "Kayy, I don't want you to go to Bible school. I believe you should get a job, rub shoulders with the world, and study at night." Thus he punctured my dream of breezing through Bible school. He firmly believed that Bible training should be done in the local church, coupled with Christian work experience. Then, as the person proved his ministry, he could be set aside for full-time work in the call of God.

Such a long process didn't appeal to me, but I finally agreed. "All right, Lord, if this is your will I'll go by the pastor's advice." I registered in our evening Bible college program, and found a job as a dental assistant with the city of Vancouver. The job paid well, with many fringe benefits. Days were boring and drab, but evenings and weekends were what I lived for.

A preacher friend, Violet Kiteley, took me under her wing for skid row mission work. The men called Violet "Dynamite," and I was "Little Dynamite." It was good experience for a would-be preacher to learn to take rebuff, to learn how to keep people from falling asleep, to see how the other side of the world lives, to learn to appreciate the problems, fears, and joys of others. There were street meetings, and these were a great training ground for learning how to lift up one's voice like a trumpet and preach the gospel of Jesus Christ.

I was just eighteen when Dorothy Williams, an accomplished Bible teacher, felt it on her heart to start a work in the town of Abbotsford, a town some forty miles southeast of Vancouver near the U.S. border. To my surprise, she invited me to join her in this new branch church. What a challenge! Twice a week, after working in the dental office all day, I'd drive with Dorothy the hour-and-a-half out to Abbotsford. The Odd Fellows' Hall was the only place available, and many people felt we were very odd indeed as we pioneered in that city with the message of revival, praise, and the moving of God's Spirit. We knocked on doors, gave out pamphlets, and shouted over loudspeakers, advertising the meetings. Our theme song was, "There's Revival in the Air Today."

But still, in all this busy challenging life of working, studying and ministering, I felt a vacuum deep inside. What was my purpose in life? What contribution could I make to humanity? Oh, just to find the perfect will of God! The future seemed so hazy. Why couldn't I share the same interests as my peers? Most of my friends were interested in their jobs, their future education, their boyfriends, hoping to find a husband and start a Christian home. But for me? Why did I have this strange compelling drive, a desire that burned like a fire to accomplish something for God?

At times I felt so restless and frustrated. "Why? Why, Lord?" A thousand times the question arose. What was it all about? It seemed as if I was just racing my motor and spinning my wheels working as a dental assistant and co-pastoring a small work at Abbotsford. Was this the only contribution that God wanted me to make?

Why was God so silent? Didn't He realize I had abandoned my

15

lifelong dream of becoming a lawyer, hoping to become a preacher? Actually, I thought I was doing Him a great service by dedicating my life to His work. No wonder the Lord couldn't speak further to me; my priorities were so topsy-turvy.

How I would chafe inwardly when Pastor Layzell would expound repeatedly about the devastating effects that pride and selfish ambition brought to our lives. How it would sting! Proud, yes. Ambitious, yes.

"But is it so wrong to be ambitious, Lord? Oh, God, help me, break me, make me," was my continual prayer.

CHAPTER 3

Alone with a Vision

The wheels of God turn slowly, but surely. By responding to a call for rededication of my life to God's service, the breaking of the ice finally came. "You're willing to be an evangelist, Kayy. But would you be willing to give your life for a few on a remote island?" God challenged my heart. This jarred my being. After three weeks of an inward struggle, I finally said "Yes, but where, Lord?"

Soon after, while praying one Saturday night, I envisioned myself in the land of ice and snow going from place to place ministering to Eskimo people. Floods of joy and gratitude flowed over my soul making sleep virtually impossible. "Lord, if this is your perfect will, let there be a lengthy emphasis on arctic needs during the Sunday services," I prayed.

This was a pretty big fleece for me to put out because at that time, our church was focusing on the field of Taiwan as our primary missionary endeavor. Unexpectedly, Pastor Layzell announced that the hour-long broadcast Sunday evening would feature a unique appeal to assist a missionary pilot, Don Violette, to purchase a plane to reach the Eskimo people in the western Arctic. I was ecstatic with joy. God had granted me the confirmation I needed. Surely my feet would soon be on the snowy terrain of Eskimo land.

Eagerly, I went to Pastor Layzell to tell him of God's call. After listening patiently to my story, he replied, "Well, Kayy, God knows your address and phone number. When He wants you, He'll call you." With this he stood up and thanked me for sharing my vision with him.

I walked out of his office stunned, with bitter tears of disappointment running down my cheeks. Little did I know that this was only a foretaste of the response and even ridicule I would continue to receive from friends and relatives for three long years. Even my dear mother, who believed in me as no one else did, could not accept this as God's will for my life.

To my utter amazement, my friends couldn't understand that God had called me to reach the Eskimo people north of the Arctic Circle with the gospel. For several months, as Dorothy and I traveled back and forth to Abbotsford, the main topic of conversation in the car was "this foolishness about Kayy going to the Arctic."

I had to learn to stand alone for the vision of reaching Eskimo people. Unknown to me, this was actually the hand of God strengthening me for the days and years of isolation that were to follow in the Arctic. No matter what people said, I still talked Arctic, read Arctic, ate Arctic, and slept Arctic. My whole being was consumed with that passion and desire to do God's will and answer His call.

The desire to go north grew brighter and stronger. I remember so well one time driving alone to Abbotsford with the burden of the Eskimos weighing so heavily on my heart that tears blurred my vision, and I had to pull off to the side of the road.

"Lord, lay Eskimos upon my heart and love their souls through me," I prayed over and over. I sang and wept. Sometimes in despair, I prayed to God that this passion inside me would die, but it only burned brighter. It was there day and night.

In those days of trials and testings, little things often were my greatest source of encouragement. An example of this was the newspaper clipping showing a person sitting on top of the world. I quickly cut out the picture and under the "Top of the World" caption, I wrote, "By faith, June, 1953." I put this in the front part of my wallet to be a constant reminder. When no one else would understand, when all reason to hope seemed to be snatched from me, this little clipping would inspire me to still believe, and dare to stand upon the promises of an unfailing God.

After three long years of fruitless efforts, I made one last trip to the pastor's office. He finally conceded to let me go, *if* someone would accompany me. Enthusiasm sparked anew. After all, who wouldn't want to go? Surely many would be delighted, given the opportunity, to venture into our northland of ice and snow. But on every hand I received only negative reactions. Desperation set into my heart and I experienced a frustration that was beyond words. "Lord, where can I find someone to share this vision?" I prayed.

Then I remembered Ken, a young man from eastern Canada with an intense desire to serve God. We had corresponded briefly following his visit to Vancouver. Surely Ken would know someone down east who would be willing to go with me, so I wrote him. "I don't know of anyone, Kayy," he answered, "but I might be interested in going myself."

For a time, the letters flew back and forth, and then Ken's letters became fewer and less frequent. Finally, I had to accept the realization that he had other interests, that the north did not burn in his heart as it did in mine. My ways and my efforts had failed again, miserably.

Pastor Layzell had heard of this correspondence with Ken. He finally realized that "Go north, young woman, go north" was ringing in my heart. He also knew that it would not be silenced, that there was a "must needs go to the Arctic" ruling in my soul.

Calling me to his office one day he startled me by saying, "All right, Kayy, get ready. You'll go as our missionary, fully supported by Glad Tidings Missionary Society."

I walked out of his office on air—no, on ice. I could almost feel those arctic winds swirling around. I could almost see the midnight sun in all its blaze of glory. I could almost taste that first reindeer steak. I could almost reach out and touch the hands of those people for whom I had been praying these three long, disappointing, frustrating years.

But then my pastor had second thoughts. Reason dictated to him that it was not wise to send a twenty-two-year-old woman alone into the wild, unknown northern wilderness—especially one with such a limited knowledge of worldly ways and the wiles of the enemy. As he drove to the office with his co-pastor, Maureen Gaglardi, he finally concluded, "We can't let Kayy go north without some definite contact. But how can we tell her this?"

God heard that conversation and, in His great foreknowledge, was working out a plan that would satisfy the reasonable concern of Pastor Layzell. That morning, walking the streets of Vancouver were two new Christians who were looking for fellowship. This dedicated couple, Anna and Mikkel Pulk, had spent the past thirty years in the Canadian Arctic. When they came to our church with its large neon sign out front that read, "Jesus Saves," they concluded, "these people must be real Christians."

At that very moment, the Spirit of God impressed on Pastor Layzell that strangers from the northland were arriving at the church.

He went to the foyer and greeted the couple coming in off the street. He astounded Mikkel and Anna by saying, "You people are from the Arctic, aren't you?"

The Pulks wondered how in the world could he know? They were just two white people wearing no parkas or mukluks. Pastor Layzell proceeded to tell them of a young woman in his assembly who had a great desire and call from God to minister among the Eskimo people.

"She must come and stay with us at Reindeer Station," the Pulks enthusiastically offered. So instead of my pastor telling me I could not go north, his voice over the phone said, "Kayy, can you hurry over here straight from work? There are two people from the Arctic I want you to meet."

How gracious the Lord is as He looks deep into the hearts of His children, and sees their innermost desires and wishes! ". . . how well he understands us, and knows what is best for us at all times" (Eph. 1:8, TLB).

CHAPTER 4

Anna and Mikkel

That evening I learned how Anna and Mikkel had come to the Canadian Arctic from their native Lapland. In an effort to stave off the dreaded years of famine that so often struck the small Eskimo groups scattered across the barrens, the Canadian government decided to bring in three thousand reindeer from Buckland Bay, Alaska. Mikkel who was a very proficient, cross-country skier able to stand many long hours driving the reindeer joined the trek in the third year as the herd neared the Canadian boundary.

The incredible endurance and courage of this small band of Lapp and Eskimo herders is incomparable. The struggle to bring these three thousand reindeer from Alaska to the Mackenzie Delta—a distance of 1800 treacherous miles—was almost inhuman. The epic trek took five years through bitter cold, howling winds, and other extreme hardships—surely the most difficult circumstances on earth.

At one time the herd was stranded on an island and the wind had swept the ice clear, making it glare ice. The reindeer were unable to walk, and were scarcely able to stand on the glassy smooth surface.

Something had to be done, but what? Ingeniously, the herders took their hatchets, and working feverishly day and night, chipped away a path for the precious reindeer to cross over.

During that same nightmarish expedition, there was a musk ox battle, when the love to kill seemed to overcome some of the Eskimo herders. In a savage battle during a storm, they attacked and killed several musk oxen. But one of the Eskimo men also perished.

Another problem was the wolves that constantly attacked the reindeer. Sometimes the wolves would sneak in during a storm, making it almost impossible to safeguard the herd.

The weather was a constant foe. Storms raging unmercifully, with fierce winds, whirling snow, angry blizzards—these were the continual lot of the brave men who undertook this great project.

Human endurance was tested to the limit. One herder knew what it was to be lost without food, to ravenously grab a lean rabbit, tear off the skin, and eat some of the raw meat in an effort to stave off the insatiable pangs of hunger. But Mikkel and his companions had a love for the reindeer that made the men fearlessly and courageously defend the deer. And so they were able to bring the herd successfully across the wild mountains, over the treacherous rivers, until at last they crossed the great Mackenzie River.

Anna had waited in Reindeer Station with their three small children. At the end of one year the herd had not arrived. There was no word. No one knew where they were or how they were progressing. Still Anna waited.

Those years were very difficult for her. She lived among Eskimo families, unable to speak their language, unable to speak even English. It was difficult to rear three small children without their father in these circumstances. But Anna was a very strong young woman. She remained undaunted by these difficulties, faithful to her husband and family. Day by day she set about to do the things a good mother and wife should do for her family. Never did she doubt that her Mikkel would one day cross the great Mackenzie and deliver the herd to Reindeer Station, just a few miles east of the delta.

Anna loved Mikkel very much, even though prior to his conversion he had been a heavy drinker and later an alcoholic. Sometimes, during the herders' drunken orgies in their unsaved days, Anna even feared for her life. More than once she had dashed outside without her parka in the sub-zero night and hidden among the willows until the tempest of the men's passions had passed.

Anna told me of her conversion. Although in the Arctic at that time the two prominent religions were Roman Catholic and Anglican, Anna had been baptized a Lutheran and she planned to stay a Lutheran. Nothing would sway her.

But one day at Reindeer Station, a small plane circled the village. Finally the plane landed and out stepped a tall, impressive stranger, a missionary from Aklavik. He handled his plane like a true pro; and yet there was something very gentle about this man's mannerisms, something very deep and penetrating about his eyes as he made the customary greeting in the north, shaking hands with every man, woman, boy and girl in sight.

Anna was rather suspicious of this stranger, more so when she learned that he was a Pentecostal minister, Don Violette. But with true northern hospitality, she invited him to visit her home and have a cup of tea. Anna waited for him to begin preaching at her, but it didn't happen. He was gracious and kind; in no way did he try to urge his convictions upon her. After a short visit, Don rose to leave, simply inviting the Pulks to attend a house meeting that evening. "There's something compelling and drawing about this man," Anna thought as he left. "I wonder what he has to say."

As the time drew near for the house meeting in a little log shack, the Eskimo people gathered together, sitting on boxes, chairs, and on the floor. Anna slipped in the door and sat at the back, impressed with the simplicity and sincerity of the service. After some singing, Don gave a very brief gospel message and then invited his listeners to accept Jesus Christ. Laura Kangegana, one of the Eskimo wives, responded and dropped to her knees on the bare boards of the cabin floor, tearfully singing, *"Omatimnon, Kain omatimnon Atanik"* which means, "Come into my heart, Lord Jesus." There was a sense of awe and wonderment about the service; then suddenly it was over and the people dispersed.

Anna thought, "I must go and see this woman. I want to see what a woman is like who has just been saved. Is there anything to it? Does it make a difference? Is it real?"

After visiting with Laura, Anna was convinced that new peace had come to her friend's heart. Laura was in the middle of severe marital problems and was just about ready to take the children and leave home. Now she had a new faith and a new strength.

"Anna, I'm going to pray for Silas and when he is saved our home will be happy," Laura radiantly affirmed. Anna shuffled home slowly over the hard-packed snow, feeling it crackle under her feet. Her mind was whirling as she wondered how these things could be.

The next night another gospel service was announced. It seemed as if an inward force compelled Anna to go again. This time there was no room in the little shack, and proud Anna, the only white woman in attendance, humbled herself to crawl under a table so that she could remain in the service and hear another message. Unnoticed, Anna listened intently.

Under the table, the fires of the Holy Spirit's conviction gripped her heart. After the simple, short sermon had been delivered, again an invitation was given for those who wanted to commit their lives to Jesus Christ. Something irresistible came over Anna, and she knew that God's call was resounding in her spirit. Others responded, and then to the astonishment of all in the room, the white lady crawled on all fours from under the table to kneel in the little space available and give her heart to Jesus Christ.

Anna became a new creature in Christ. "Old things passed

away"—the old fears, the old hatreds—and "all things became new" for her in Christ. From that day until the time of her death, Anna's direction in life was only one way—for God!

Anna's great concern for the Eskimos matured as the years passed. Time after time she would pray for Eskimo couples. She named them before the Lord, asking that they might love each other, and love God above all. How they loved her, especially in her later years!

When I met the Pulks that Friday evening in our church office in Vancouver, little did I realize what a great help this older couple would be to me in my arctic ministry. They too were equally amazed when they met me, for somehow they expected an older person, bigger and more robust. But they were gracious, and told me what I would need to begin living in the north. It was fascinating to me and so thrilling, so exciting. At last the dream of my life was about to be fulfilled.

After a couple of hours' discussion, as Mikkel and Anna were leaving, Anna told me very coyly about her son at Reindeer Station. She described him as a blond, twenty-five-year-old bachelor who "looked like the Duke of Edinburgh." Later on, as we set the date for my arrival in the Arctic, again Anna made mention of her son Nels, and it began to dawn on me that she perhaps had some thoughts that the "duke" and I would "hit it off." Later on she confessed to me that indeed she had felt like Eliezer, the servant, in the story of Rebekah and Isaac. This rather amused me, but when I eventually met Nels, I found that he had other ideas. His mind and heart were full of a beautiful young Eskimo girl he planned to marry.

Into the North

CHAPTER 5

My Promised Land

The days seemed to fly by as I prepared to go to the Arctic, but in the midst of my excitement there was a burden—the concern for my sick and aging mother. Although not totally an invalid, mother was on crutches. We had been so close since the death of my father. I loved my mom, and it hurt a great deal to have to leave her. My decision to go into the Arctic and leave mother was made after long deliberation, with many nights tearfully spent. But that consuming passion to do God's will had to have preeminence.

Strangely enough, a few months before this I had a telephone call from mother's Christian doctor, telling me that mother's multiple sclerosis was incurable (as we had known), and that it would be slowly degenerative. He went on to talk to me about my own future. "Live your own life," he counseled. "Don't give up your life to stay with your mother. She'll be all right." His words rather angered me, but I tried to appear composed. Again he repeated, "Kayy, if you give up your plans and ambitions to stay home to look after your mother, you'll lose what you hope to gain.''

In the succeeding months I reflected upon his words, and began to wonder if Dr. Fraser had not been guided by the Lord to give me advice in this very sensitive area. Naturally it was a blow to mom. She wanted me to preach the gospel, but in her heart she had always secretly hoped that we could stay together and that she could travel with me wherever I might preach. When she saw my mind was steadfastly set to go north, mother was very gracious, and courageously tried to make the best of it. Her indomitable spirit that had kept her fighting multiple sclerosis for fifteen years rose up as she determined to make my last two weeks pleasant ones so I could leave with happy memories.

A week before my departure, an unexpected letter arrived from a sister-in-law in eastern Canada. She was upset that I was leaving mother. The family felt that it was a very foolish move which would only end in heartache and trouble. She proceeded to tell me how ungrateful I was to leave my mom, how I could do God's will looking after her, how religion must begin at home and how very disappointed they were with my decision.

I read the letter carefully. Then realizing that she just didn't understand, I prayed for each member of my family, that God would bring them to a place of knowing that the greatest thing in this life is to do God's will. I wanted them to know that being where He wants us to be, doing what He wants us to do, and being all we should be for the Lord are the purposes of life. Then I took the letter and carefully ripped it to shreds and burned it, lest by keeping it in my possession I might reread it and become bitter, or be unduly troubled by it. Again I was forced to realize that I must stand alone in the convictions and purposes of my faith, not letting any of these things dissuade me, but keeping before me a clear vision of reaching Eskimos.

Misunderstandings and discouragements—was there no end to them? I began to wonder. And then I realized that this is the way it is in life. These things are destined to happen to everybody. It's not so much what happens to us that counts; it's how we react to the things that happen. A wonderful assurance from within surged up again and I knew that all would be well if I obeyed God's call.

Each morning I awoke with a sort of insecure feeling. "What might happen today? If only I can get through today without another negative." I noticed mother was becoming quieter as the days went by. Some mornings her eyes revealed her quiet sufferings as she realized that soon "the apple of her eye" would leave her. These things hurt deeply but we didn't discuss them. We were both trying to adjust to our new lots in life.

There were fun things to do—like going downtown to buy heavy underwear. The salesgirls would look at me with astonishment when I asked them for their heaviest, thickest Stanfield long johns. In the month of June!

"You must be going to the sticks," one said.

"No, I'm going beyond the sticks," I answered.

The ladies missionary band wanted to give me a gift. "Could you use flannel sheets?" they asked.

"That's a wonderful idea. Can they be grey flannel?" I enthused, thinking of the months of roughing it ahead.

They seemed rather embarrassed to make such a presentation, but what a blessing those grey flannel sheets proved to be in musty, dusty tents.

The night came for my farewell service at the little church in Abbotsford. As we met, I suddenly began to realize that I was leaving them all. But the joy of reaching out and doing the will of God far exceeded the sorrow of being separated from those who meant so much to me. The people of this church where I had co-pastored with Dorothy were so gracious to me. In this newly established church there was a glad response to my entering the mission field.

Finally, my last day in Vancouver rolled around—Friday, June 15, 1956. As I preached my last service in my home church, the full impact that I was really leaving hit me. How could I say good-bye to this happy fellowship of wonderful people. The warmth and love flowing from that dear congregation toward me provided a memory that lived and relived in my heart a hundred times over. In the years to come, when the going was tough and progress so slow, I would think about that last service together, and I would again feel the warmth of their love and concern. This memory never ceased to inspire me, to lift me up above the shadows into the great sky of faith.

I was to spend the weekend in a church in Edmonton, then proceed northward very early Monday morning. Our friends, the Browns, met me at Edmonton International Airport and their hospitality was so welcome as the time of separation from loved ones and friends began to pain deeply. Over the years I had developed an attitude that it was a sign of weakness to show emotion, particularly the emotion of sorrow. So I fixed my face in a smile and bore up, with the anticipation of the future ever before me—that vision of Kayy Gordon sitting on top of the world.

We had a good Sunday in the Wells of Joy Church, and then at about five o'clock Monday morning, I awakened. The long-awaited day had arrived. Not knowing what to expect, I pulled on long underwear, one pair of socks, and a second pair of slacks because I had no room left in my suitcase. In addition, I wore a flannelette shirt, a boy's leather jacket, big boots and mitts. Little did I realize that it was beautifully warm in the Arctic during these days of twenty-four-hour sunshine, and that all my precautions against possible cold were needless.

The old DC-4 that was going to fly us on the "milk run" from Edmonton to Norman Wells revved up and with a few creaks and groans rolled down the runway. Finally we were airborne, flying over prairie, then bush scattered with lakes. We were headed "down north." My heart beat faster in my youthful zeal, knowing that my Utopia was just ahead.

Hour after hour we traveled in this old plane. We crossed Great Slave Lake, with its east arm still iced over. Along the Mackenzie,

I could see the tree line falling away to the east where the forbidding grey rocks and tundra and shallow ponds stretched far in the distance.

Finally, after about eight hours, we reached Norman Wells, the oil-producing center where that early explorer, Alexander Mackenzie, first noticed oil seeping from the river banks. Twenty-seven wells are in production there and they supply the whole western Arctic. The refineries turn out everything except jet fuel.

But I wasn't interested in the oil. My heart was wrapped up in the ''treasures of the snow''—the people of that frozen land still in darkness without the light of the gospel. I jumped off the plane, eagerly anticipating the community, the village . . . something! I'll never forget the feeling of desolation that enveloped me as I looked around. The airport was miles from town; there was virtually nothing—just a few trees and hills. A small group of natives and whites were waiting for the smaller Twin Otter that would fly us beyond the Arctic Circle to the village of Aklavik on the western edge of the Mackenzie River Delta.

As we boarded the aircraft, I noticed that I was the only woman in the group, and this set the pattern for the future also. In the north, I moved in circles where there were mostly men, and this just became a way of life. In these small planes, passengers, baggage and freight all share the same area. The center aisle is piled high with luggage, crates and bags. Once you're belted in, that's it for the trip.

On down the river we flew, with the mountains to the east and west of us. About eight o'clock, someone said we were coming into Aklavik. Eagerly I looked out the window to catch my first glimpse of this big settlement. I was somewhat taken aback to see dozens and dozens of houses built from drift logs, muddy streets, straggling wooden sidewalks, and in general, a very unkempt looking town. ''Well,'' I thought, ''this is the Arctic and this is the way it is, so never mind.''

As we circled Aklavik, I suddenly had the disconcerting thought that Anna Pulk would not be there to meet me.

"Oh, yes, she will," I argued with myself. "She told me she would meet the plane."

But something within me said, "Be prepared. Don't be surprised. No one is going to meet you. . . ."

And, as I scanned the shores, it was true, I could see no trace of Anna. My premonition had been correct, and my heart sank.

I took a long time to gather my things together, not wanting to be the first one off the plane. Finally, the men gave up the idea of being gentlemen and climbed down onto the dock. As I stepped out of that plane and slowly clambered down the rickety ladder onto the float dock, I took my first step into the Arctic, alone. I didn't fully realize that this was the way it was going to be, that often in the future I would have to face things alone in my ministry to the north.

A wave of loneliness hit me. This was just a preliminary of something every northerner must learn to cope with. Not just minutes of loneliness nor hours, but long days, weeks and sometimes months.

As casually as possible, I stepped off the float dock and those brown faces that smiled so sweetly at me certainly gave me a feeling of reassurance. Not knowing what else to do, I smiled back and tightened up the belt of my leather jacket, took a deep breath and said, "All right, Lord, what do I do now?" Everyone dispersed quickly from the plane and I was left on the shore alone except for the mosquitoes, the dust and the mud. A small wave of despair rolled over me. "That's foolish," I thought. "There's got to be a way and I'll just have to find it." I noticed two young native girls standing along the bank.

"Could you tell me where Otto and Ellen Binder live?" I asked. This was Anna's daughter and son-in-law and I was to stay with them.

"Sure, we'll take you there," they readily responded—in

English! So, with typical northern grace and hospitality, the girls not only directed me to the home, but personally took me to the door. And who should open the door but Anna! Her face looked so good to me and I was so relieved, for I knew there was no hotel that was decent to stay in. I knew no one else. But now I was in the house of friends.

Anna apologized profusely for not meeting the plane. She had been confused as to the time of its arrival. No matter. The main thing was that I had made contact. I was with someone I knew, someone who cared.

The home of her daughter and son-in-law was small, sparsely furnished, yet friendly and welcoming to this young stranger. They seemed amused that I was so young. Actually, I didn't look twenty-two. I weighed scarcely 105 pounds, and had to stand on tiptoe to reach five feet three inches. There was nothing about me that suggested either strength or endurance. Undoubtedly the thought crossed the minds of these rugged northerners: "How long will this kid last?"

Ellen and Otto were Roman Catholic in belief, but northern hospitality reaches beyond denominationalism, creed or dogma. In the north, people are people. They share with each other, because one day they may need the other person to share with them. Utter interdependence is a very real part of northern life.

Ellen made tea and decided I must be hungry, so she quickly whipped up a meal. "Do you eat reindeer meat?" she asked.

"Well, I never tasted it, but I sure would like to," I replied. As I took my first mouthful of reindeer meat, its wildness and strong flavor filled every part of my mouth. But, in my heart, I said, "This is Eskimo food. This I am going to like!" I took another bite.

"How do you like it?" they asked curiously.

"Oh, I like it!" I exclaimed. I spoke from my heart, even if my taste buds did not momentarily agree.

As I sat at that little wooden table with its faded oilcloth, and looked down at the badly worn linoleum-covered floor, I realized I would need to make the adjustment to not only accept, but enjoy, simple living. After finishing the delicious meal of thick slices of homemade bread, canned butter and jam, reindeer steak and pickles, washed down with big cups of tea, I settled back to enjoy a little time of conversation with this northern household.

Ellen Binder was obviously a very well-read person. I was amazed to find that she had only a sixth grade formal education. She had read every book in the Aklavik library—the "heavies" as well as the novels. Her vocabulary was more developed than many people whom I associated with in the south.

When Ellen was only fourteen years old she had married Otto, a part-Eskimo man, and she had created a happy home with her husband and five children. A stunning Lappish girl with a vibrant personality and a great deal of ability, Ellen understood the thinking of Eskimo people, perhaps better than almost anyone else whom I had the privilege to encounter.

As we talked together, I couldn't resist the temptation to go frequently to the window and stare out at those beautiful skies. It was a late evening in mid-June, yet the sun was circling the horizon in the brightness of noonday glory. The sun never sets at that time of year, and the entire sky was blazing with hues of red and gold. I was fascinated. Such a feeling of exhilaration came over me as for the first time I enjoyed the wonder of the midnight sun.

At about eleven o'clock, Anna announced that I would be staying in another home with a nurse friend of hers. Ellen's home was obviously already overcrowded with her five children, her parents, and grandparents. Somehow I didn't want to leave the security of Ellen's home, but I got my things together and started down the muddy road to the nurse's house. Although well past midnight, the village was still buzzing with activity. The children were playing in the streets and the women were hanging clothes on a line. Many people were just getting up.

During the long summer days, often the Eskimos stay up at night hunting, fishing, working, visiting, and then they sleep most of the day. Days turn to night and nights to day very quickly in the Arctic during the summer season. As we walked along the wooden sidewalks, past dingy little log cabins, often half-dressed children popped out of the doors. They always had that little smile, so characteristic of the Eskimo people.

My new hostess was Winnie, an English nurse who had spent two years or more in Aklavik. She had come to the place of a fuller commitment of her life to Christ at Aklavik. Consequently, she was misunderstood by some of her friends and working associates. It's not an easy row to hoe, to stand alone for one's convictions. This has broken many a person in the north.

We shared a few things, and then Winnie suggested we go next door to visit the missionary and his wife, Don and Gladys Violette. "Don't you think it's a little late?" I asked. It was now after one o'clock. Winnie just smiled. "You'll learn the ways of the north in a little while," she counseled.

We went next door and, after introductions, I was soon aware that the Violettes too wondered about the advisability of my coming into the north. I sensed a question that was being asked in their hearts and minds—"How long will this kid last?" Everyone seemed so unsure of me, questioning my motives and my call from God to the ministry in the Arctic.

Later that night, as I lay in bed unable to sleep because of the rays of the sun still streaming through the window, I realized that I would have to prove myself in everything relating to my northern ministry. It would be required of me to "make full proof my ministry." It was very clear to me that I would not be accepted until I had done this.

So from day one and hour one in my arctic living, I had to learn to totally trust the Lord, to make Jesus Christ not only my Savior and Lord, but also He had to become my close friend. He had to be "the lifter up of mine head" (Ps. 3:3). He had to be the strength of my life. He must become my all in all.

I was awakened mid-morning by the excited announcement, "The Moose is coming!" The "Moose" turned out to be a large scow-type government boat coming from Reindeer Station to Aklavik for a visit, piloted by Charlie Smith, the Eskimo leader at Reindeer Station. There was a great deal of excitement as the Moose came into view, for this was its first trip of the summer into Aklavik. I too was eager to meet these reindeer herders.

Charlie Smith, a small, middle-aged man, his happy face weathered by arctic winds, gave me the warmest greeting anyone had given to me up to this time. When he learned I was a missionary, Charlie immediately began to share his faith in Jesus. I felt a bond of understanding with this Eskimo man. How wonderful it is to belong to the family of God! In Jesus Christ, the color of our skin doesn't matter one bit. Charlie's first mate was another reindeer herder, Danny Sidney. Danny was very shy and quiet, but he too loved the Lord. I marveled as I watched them maneuver their boat around the dock to a landing spot. They worked with such ease and skill.

The Moose would be returning to Reindeer Station the next day, but because they had just arrived, there would be a service that night with the Aklavik Christians. It's the Eskimo custom, whenever Christian visitors arrive in town, to hold a special service in order to rejoice in the good things of God together.

The service that night was to be in the house of an Alaskan-born Eskimo, Charlie Gordon. His father was a white man, his mother an Eskimo, and Charlie Gordon became a strong Eskimo leader. He and his wife, Thea, had come from Alaska and settled in Aklavik some years before.

It was a great day in the north when the gospel of Jesus Christ reached this couple. Some years earlier, Don Violette had been ministering in Aklavik and had invited anyone who had any questions to remain after the service. Thea stayed and asked him a soul-searching question: "I've been looking for Jesus Christ, but I cannot find Him. Can you help me?'' What a joy it was for Don to lead this woman to the Christ for whom she had been searching.

A deep work was done in Thea, and, in a short time, Charlie also came to know Jesus Christ. Charlie had been quite a hard-drinking man who led a fast life. But what an exciting transformation the power of the gospel makes in the Eskimos as they turned literally from darkness to light! Now Charlie Gordon had become an Eskimo leader in the church and the service was to be in his little log shack.

A shack indeed it was, very tiny. Yet eight or ten people—babies, grandchildren, sons and daughters-in-law—were all living in the sparsely furnished house. Somehow, another thirty crowded in and we had a service by gas lamp. Charlie Smith from Reindeer Station testified, his face aglow as he told of the wonderful change Jesus Christ had made in his life. The room temperature must have risen to about 90 degrees but no one thought to turn the oil heater down. Everybody was sweating. Soon the air was pungent with perspiration odor. In the heat, the sealskin boots began to give off their own special aroma and the fur parkas did likewise. But I seemed to be the only one aware of these things. Their hearts and minds were looking heavenward. Their spirits were reaching out to God. The simplicity and depth of their devotion left an impression on my heart that I shall never forget. When they prayed for others, there was such a compassion, such feeling, such meaning. No one could doubt the sincerity of those Eskimo Christians, still so young in the faith.

I just sat there enthralled by it all, striving to understand the strange words I was hearing, and wondering if I could ever learn to speak the Eskimo language. I prayed that God would somehow give me ears to hear and a mouth to speak, and a heart that would understand.

When the service ended, a time of fellowship began. A few of the younger ones went outside, but even in that hot, uncomfortable environment almost everyone stayed. Tonight there was going to be a special treat of Eskimo ice cream. Would I try it? Sure I would! Suddenly they set before me a dishful of something that looked a bit like soft ice cream, but, to my dismay, I found that it was a dish of caribou fat with pieces of dried caribou and fish mixed in. As I began to eat, I must admit I had to pray for grace. Mouthful upon mouthful of fat was very foreign to me. How will I ever get it all down, I wondered. But I did. That was my first introduction to Eskimo delicacies!

Because of the limited facilities in Eskimo homes, it was very difficult to have any standards of sanitation. When tea was made, everyone was welcome to have a ''belly-wash,'' as Charlie called it. It was impossible to wash every cup between users, so you learned to turn the cup around until you came to an area that didn't appear to have been used. But all these things were incidental. The spirit of grace and love among these people was so warming and so beautiful that I could soon overlook the undersirable elements.

We were to leave the next morning for Reindeer Station. In my ignorance I thought that meant *early* the next morning, so I was up and ready by eight o'clock. Well, Eskimo time is a little different from our time. Nine o'clock passed. Ten o'clock passed. By eleven, some were just getting up. About two in the afternoon we were ready to leave. Anna and I, along with the Eskimos who had brought the Moose down the Mackenzie to Aklavik, stood on the deck, waving good-bye to those on the shore. We were finally on our way.

The Moose was a very slow-moving boat and the trip would take about eight hours. Traveling down the Mackenzie in June is a beautiful experience, with birds calling and flying over the low willows, stretches of golden sand along the shoreline, and grassy meadows that shelter the most prolific muskrat colony on the continent. This great wilderness held many secrets of God's handiwork, and it seemed to call out to us as we passed. But my interest was not to explore the depths of nature. How I longed to explore the depths of Eskimo life and feelings and actions, that I might be a blessing to them in some way.

The sun was dazzling and I found it hard to believe that we were north of the Arctic Circle. As the day grew warm we took off our jackets. Anna pulled out a little Coleman stove, pumped and lit it, and made some coffee. Then she brought out a hindquarter of reindeer meat and began hacking off pieces, tossing them in the frying pan. Soon a tasty meal was ready for us. If an Eskimo can have meat, it's a happy day, and reindeer meat seemed to be featured that day, for breakfast, lunch and supper. We passed the time talking, singing gospel songs, resting, and eating more reindeer meat. It was a truly happy day!

We turned off the Mackenzie into another channel and suddenly Anna exclaimed, "There it is—Reindeer Station!" Straining my eyes, in the distance I could see a few small dots along the shore in a beautiful setting among the hills, just barely within the tree line.

As we neared the settlement, I could make out a dozen or so little log buildings clustered together within a small radius. Closer, I heard the howl of the dogs, the signal in the north that someone is arriving. Eskimos, big and small, came running out of the houses. By the time the Moose was docked, every person in the settlement seemed to be on hand.

This was a big event. It had been the Moose's first trip to Aklavik that summer and we were coming back with all kinds of goodies and supplies on board. The first barges from the south had just previously arrived at Aklavik so the children knew we'd have apples and oranges on board. The women were anxiously anticipating mail orders they had sent for months earlier. The men were eager for the new outboard motors, the canoes and speedboats that should be on board. Interest was high as everyone pitched in to help unload the boat.

How can I describe my feeling of adventure and excitement as I arrived in Reindeer Station this first time? These were the people I would be living with for the next year.

After shaking hands with everyone on the shore and helping

unload the boat, we finally made our way to a little log shack set apart from the others. This was Anna and Mikkel's simple home. In one corner was a couch that had seen better days; opposite it was an upholstered chair covered by an Indian-type blanket. There were kitchen cupboards, a cookstove, table and chairs, but no running water. Their bedroom was just large enough for a bed and dresser, and another tiny corner was partitioned off for the famous northern "honey bucket" (an indoor toilet of sorts with a disposable plastic bag).

At Reindeer Station I was rapidly introduced to something else that was new and almost unbelievable. Thick swarms of mosquitoes hummed and buzzed around everyone, making the air almost black with their presence. It was impossible to be outdoors without massive amounts of mosquito repellent on every exposed area of the body. It seemed unfair in this region, where one fights the severe winter weather, that the short summer season should be plagued with these swarming mosquitoes. They usually last at Reindeer Station for about five weeks until the winds begin to blow in July.

During mosquito season, the children suffer terribly and are afflicted with appalling cases of impetigo as a result of scratching mosquito bites. Later on that fall we were in a herd camp where one five-year-old girl had developed a severe case. The bites had become infected and had spread all over little Mildred's body. She was in utter misery, her face swollen to twice its normal size. It was the "freeze-up season" and we were immobilized; no communication was available with the doctor or nurse. Traveling was impossible. There was nothing we could do but pray.

Laura, the mother, had a tremendous faith in God. "God will heal my child," she confidently declared. We prayed together, and I returned to my tent very concerned.

The next morning I was almost afraid to return to Laura's tent and little Mildred. To my amazement, the child had improved considerably; her swelling had gone down and the impetigo was beginning to dry up. Laura was not surprised but just smiled and with a glow about her said, "God did heal my child, and He will make her completely better." Within two or three days all the running sores had healed, and after a week they were completely dried up, leaving no scars. She had been completely healed because of her mother's faith.

The mosquitoes are also a dreadful plague to the dogs. All summer long, while they are not being used, the dogs are tied to a stake on a three- or four-foot chain. They have no defense against the hordes of mosquitoes. Often long into the night their tortured howls and yelps are heard.

This first evening at the station, after settling in at the Pulks, I joined them in making the rounds of the settlement, visiting in the homes, greeting one another. Suddenly the activity was disrupted by some children shouting, "The reindeer boat is coming!" They had been up on the hill behind the station and had spotted a little dot on one of the river's channels. It would take a few hours for the boat to reach Reindeer Station, but no one was planning to sleep. Everyone was anxious to see these reindeer herders who had been out in their camps for the last two months.

Finally, about one o'clock, the little reindeer boat came into view. Many people jammed its small deck. In fact, it appeared that as many as could possibly leave the herd had taken advantage of this opportunity to visit Reindeer Station. When the boat arrived, there was the customary handshake all around. What joy as they greeted each other again! They had so much to talk about.

But before they had all disappeared into their homes, Charlie Smith, the recognized leader of the people, came over to me.

"Kayy," he said, "whenever the reindeer herders return for a visit, we always have a service, and tonight we'd like one so they can all meet you. Would that be all right?" I was delighted. This was surely unique, preparing for a service in the middle of the night! After "supper," these Christian herders gathered with their Bibles at three in the morning in Charlie's little log house.

What a service it was! The depth and sincerity of their simple praise to God was beautiful, as they related the different ways the Lord had helped them and answered their prayers.

One man, Kailek, told of how during the spring move with the big Caterpillar pulling a caboose, he somehow had been caught between the Cat and the caboose. The Cat driver was unable to see him and backed up, literally squashing Kailek. When the driver pulled ahead, Kailek fell to the ground unconscious.

Many of these people had just been saved through the ministry of Don Violette, and in their new-found faith they had learned that God answers prayer. Not knowing what else to do, they gathered around Kailek and began to pray that God would help their brother. After a time of prayer, Kailek sat up and declared that he was better. Those around him said they had actually heard bones crack and snap as the Christians prayed.

They knew their boss at Reindeer Station would expect them to return with Kailek, so they did this, still confident in their hearts that God had healed him. At the boss' insistence, they rushed Kailek to Aklavik for a series of X-rays. The doctors were amazed. Some ribs had been broken and cracked, but it was clear that they had mended themselves perfectly. Kailek was pronounced totally recovered. Oh, the power of simple faith in a living God!

As for the first time I opened the Scriptures to these Eskimo people, I was very aware that while I was ministering to them, they were also ministering to me. The Lord very graciously revealed some things to me concerning needs in their lives that I had no way of knowing, except from above.

One woman came for prayer. The Lord showed me that the big problem in her life was that she had no children. The Lord gave me a word that she would bear a son before the year was over. Unknown to me, her inability to bear children had almost ruined this young couple's marriage. God watched over His word and brought it to pass, and before the next summer, she indeed gave birth to a baby boy.

These words of prophecy and the healings in those early days greatly helped the Eskimo people accept me as a spiritual leader. It was the first time they had ever seen a woman minister; but little by little they realized that God had called me to be with them and their confidence in my ministry was established.

I left that very first service in the little log house about 5:30 A.M., unable to keep my eyes open any longer. The Eskimos are a very warm, sociable people, taking a great interest in every detail of each other's lives. They would continue to visit and drink tea for another three or four hours. But I had not yet been able to switch over to their timetable.

As I fell wearily but happily into bed, I was convinced of one thing: I was certainly going to enjoy these days (and nights) with the reindeer herders!

Next day there was no activity until afternoon. Then suddenly everyone seemed to be up. The settlement was bustling with people as the reindeer herders prepared to return to their spring camp at Wolf Creek. They are constantly traveling, and it amazed me that they could do it with such ease. They can set up camp quickly, and in short, are able to come and go at a moment's notice.

In these small settlements, the Hudson's Bay store is always the meeting place. Everyone seems to converge there. The children were stocking up on goodies—chocolate bars, pop, bubble gum—and the women were shopping for their household requirements. Before long, everyone was weighted down with parcels and boxes, making their way to the dock. Just as soon as the wind dropped, they'd be off. I was to make this trip with them and I felt a growing excitement as I faced camping in the north for the first time.

Again I figured that we would be shoving off early, but there were numerous delays and finally at about eleven that night we set sail. With the little tugboat pushing the well-loaded barge, we were on our way thirty miles down the Mackenzie to Wolf Creek.

After a few hours of travel—winding in and out of different channels, stopping to chase a bear in the willows, and to make tea on the beach (any old excuse will do for a tea-stop in the north)—at last we could see a few dots in the distance. It was Wolf Creek Reindeer Camp. Even though our arrival was in the middle of the night, all those who had been left in camp were at the shore, happily welcoming home their loved ones as if they'd been away two months instead of two days.

I was beginning to realize that Eskimo people are really a very lonely people who are very dependent upon each other. It's common in the Eskimo culture to visit each other's homes every day. Particularly where the settlements are smaller, the same vistors drop in every day, and perhaps a few times a day. If they have not seen someone for a day or two, they will often remark, "I never see you for long time." Visiting is an integral part of their culture.

At Wolf Creek I helped unload the barge, carrying my things up to a little shack Mikkel and Anna had built. With rough boards for walls, rough wood on the floors, a homemade bunk at each end, a rough hewn table and a couple of chairs—this was going to be my home until the ship came again from the south with my supplies and a new tent. We settled in, had tea and reindeer meat, and then went to bed at what I learned was the usual time when traveling with the reindeer herders in summer—six in the morning.

It's amazing how quickly one can adjust to such a radical change in schedule. In just a few days' time it seemed perfectly normal for me to go to bed at six and get up at one or two in the afternoon.

The next day, after breakfast at two in the afternoon, I set out to make the rounds of the camp. In one tent I met Rhoda, an impressive young Eskimo woman, devoted to her husband and children. She bore a child almost every year, but each child was looked after and cared for in a beautiful way. Rhoda was a godly woman, saved only a few months previously. One of her children was sick, so we prayed together and God healed the child, again

48

helping to bring the Eskimo people and myself closer together.

I also met twenty-one-year-old Sophie, the only single girl who did not have children. Sophie was a quiet girl and so eager to serve God. She became very friendly and as a consequence, Sophie lived with me in the tent, and then later went with me to the village of Tuk where we spent three years together. Sophie was a fine witness to her people and a great help to me in the Lord's work.

As I went from tent to tent, a whole new way of life opened up before me. The basic living conditions of tent life are so different from life in a house. There were always so many bare-bottomed children running around, always climbing on something—the table, the beds, the bunks, and crawling over the clothes on the floor. They were always in motion.

One thing that bothered me in my first days of tent life (and continued to trouble me during my many years in the north), was the multi-purpose cloth used in many households. The same cloth would be used to dry hands, dry dishes, wipe up anything spilled on the floor, and even wipe the kids' noses. It would also be passed around after a meal to wipe every individual's hands and face. This always made me a little squeamish inside.

Later, when visiting another settlement, I was so pleased to see one housewife actually rinsing the dishes with hot water in a basin. I thought to myself, "This is really progress!" However, the next day I happened to be around when she was washing the floor with water from the same basin. Then again later that day she made *bannock* (an overgrown baking-powder pancake fried in lard in a heavy cast-iron frying pan) in it. I knew there would be different sanitary standards in every culture, yet still it was quite an adjustment for me.

A big event occurred each evening in Wolf Creek when Mikkel turned on the radio and tuned in the short-wave station from Quito, Ecuador. It was squawky, the music was distorted and we could hardly make out the words as the station faded in and out, but it was contact with the outside world and with other Christians. Soon I too was sitting by the radio desperately trying to decipher the program. No one will ever know how much those broadcasts meant to us up there in that lonely reindeer camp on the barren lands.

We had services nearly every other night and I remember so well the first time that some of the young people responded, making fresh commitments to serve God. Perhaps it was because I too was quite young. How the older ones rejoiced also each time a young person was blessed. Their joy made me realize in a little measure what Jesus meant when He told of the joy in heaven over one sinner who repents.

Much of my time was spent teaching God's Word, simply encouraging the people to go on with God, to praise Him and rejoice. They were impressed with the joy that Jesus gives. I taught them the message they wanted so much to hear about the Holy Ghost—of how they might be "endued with power from on high" and become more effective witnesses for Jesus Christ.

One time they threw me with their comment, "Kayy, don't you ever have temptations or troubles? You always seem so happy." That was almost a joke, because within my heart there were so many moments of frustration and uncertainty. But I tried to convey that faith overcomes, and that our God is the God of every circumstance.

Another trial for me personally in those early days was the direct change in life style. In Vancouver every moment seemed taken up with my job, studying, and co-pastoring the church at Abbotsford. But here my life was totally unstructured, and the hours passed so slowly. After reading and praying and visitation, what else could I do? I decided to go for a long walk, but the mosquitoes were buzzing and biting miserably. And the tundra, being spongy and full of little potholes, is not easy to walk on. You have to watch very carefully where you step or you can easily stumble and turn an ankle. So I soon abandoned that idea. There were no letters to answer because there was no mail in or out. I found it tedious to have so much time on my hands, and especially with twenty-four hours of daylight, it was even worse.

But the Eskimos delight in these long days. Often, after the service in the evenings, one of the Eskimo boys would run out of the tent and cry, "Play ball! Play ball!" There, on the pot-holed tundra, they would set up an impromptu ball diamond, the roughest imaginable. Young and old would gather to play softball, not just for an hour or two, but often from 10 P.M. until 5 A.M., with never a broken leg. The Arctic is the land of extremes and those who live in that land tend to be extremists.

Soon I could squat on reindeer skins as easily as I could sit on a chair. Cold soup, cold tea and frozen raw food were soon an everyday diet. (It took a little longer to develop a taste for caribou eyes.)

When traveling and camping for the night, I soon learned the art of just taking off my boots and parka, then lying down fully clad in the sleeping bag.

At first the idea of not having a bath was appalling, but after a few weeks this too became a normal course of events. When my own tent finally arrived, it was much easier to manage an occasional sponge bath. When the darkness finally came, I could turn out my gas lamp, strip and wash down in the dark.

Actually, it turned out to be two-and-a-half years before I'd even see a bathtub, and when that opportunity finally came, I found it cold and undesirable, not at all the pleasurable experience I had remembered. With a little water in a basin and fairly frequent sponge baths, it's not too much of a problem to keep clean without a bathtub or shower. I was pleased when a teacher commented to a mutual friend, "Somehow Kayy always looks well-scrubbed." I took that as a great compliment, because she didn't know the primitive conditions I was living in.

After a couple of weeks at Wolf Creek, one day Mikkel came with the news, "The ice is all clear." We could now move to the summer camp up on the Arctic seacoast. Everyone was excited because the camp at Kiklavak Bay was just across from the whaling station, and summertime was the time to hunt the beautiful white beluga whales.

Eagerly, the Eskimos loaded their supplies, equipment and belongings onto the barge. What a sight it was—furniture, dogs, people, children, everything imaginable taken on board the old scow. But this was the way they traveled. We'd been underway for only an hour when Mikkel gave the command to drop anchor. As an experienced seaman, he knew the winds were coming up fast across the delta and it would have been dangerous to proceed any farther with the heavily loaded barge. We anchored in a little cove and waited for the wind to die down. Hour after hour we waited.

"This is our regular service night. Why don't we have a service on board?" suggested Joe Panaktuk, a young Eskimo.

Soon he had his guitar out and everybody gathered for a time of rejoicing in God's presence. It was rather unique, this meeting on the little boat, feeling the sway from the howling winds, the waves slapping against the sides of the boat. But still the people entered into the presence of God, not permitting their circumstances to concern them.

I've always appreciated the Eskimos' ability to worship God regardless of time, place or situation. The children can be running around, the babies crying, and a great deal of commotion going on all about them; yet they seem able to turn it all off and tune in to heaven.

Following the service, we had our usual cup of tea and bite to eat, and then we dozed on the deck while we waited. For twenty-three hours we waited until finally Mikkel announced, "Let's shove off!" In a few minutes we were again heading down the Mackenzie, sailing beyond the tree line, until, at last, the familiar little specks came in sight. This time they were three or four Quonset-type huts along the shore.

The Eskimo people still preferred to live in their tents, so quickly these were set up. In a few short hours, belongings were unloaded and the whole camp was again reestablished. Children scampered off in every direction to discover new wonders about them. About five or six in the morning after the fishnets were set, the camp became totally silent as we all fell into a deep sleep, so happy to be on the shore again.

Camp was pitched right on the beach. Rolling hills of tundra behind us were now blooming wildly with many arctic flowers. The unique, compelling beauty of the Barren Grounds somehow appealed to me from the beginning. My greatest delight was to climb over a little mound away from the camp where I could view that vast, empty land rolling away as far as the eye can see. For me, this vastness brought heaven a little nearer, making me realize my own smallness and insignificance.

At Kiklavak Bay the menu was mostly fish. Our supplies of canned goods had almost run out, so each day the men would visit the nets and bring us fresh white fish. We had fish for breakfast, fish for lunch and fish for supper. After gutting the fish and cutting them in chunks, the women boiled them in a big blackened pot over their primus stove. Thirty minutes later we would fork a piece out of the pot and plunk it on our enamel plates. Then we'd go at this "finger-lickin' fish" by breaking the head, sucking out the brains and eyes. (Mmmmm—but not that first year for me.)

After a few weeks at Kiklavak the time came for the annual reindeer roundup. This was a busy season for the herders. The herd had to be brought into the corralled area to be counted, and some were castrated and earmarked. One or two government officials would come in, plus a number of Eskimo families, because extra workers were always needed.

A roundup bonus for the Eskimos was that now, after a steady diet of fish all through June and July, they would have fresh meat, because the Eskimos would be allowed to shoot some of the reindeer.

The shooting of the deer was very curious to me. About one hundred reindeer would be brought into the corral where the men would single out the ones they planned to shoot. When the first deer was shot right in the middle of the herd, I thought the rest would stampede. But the other deer simply watched as one dropped, then another and another. It struck me that this was like so many people today who seem to able to stand unmoved as they see their fellowman suffering from the circumstances of life. The attitude so often is, "Oh, well, it didn't hit me or mine."

Each evening of the reindeer roundup we had a service. The numbers were swelled by the many visitors; it was the crowning moment of each day.

On one occasion, Don Violette visited the camp and spoke on consecrating our lives for the Lord's service. Two of the Eskimo men responded, falling to their knees on the rough wood floor of the tent. I was asked to pray with them.

The one man I knew very well. He was Charlie Smith, an obvious leader, a man with much ability and potential. The other man was John Maksagak, whom I had just met. John was a quiet, sincere man with a kindly manner about him, compassionate and understanding of others. But he did not possess the noticeable qualities of leadership like Charlie. As I went to pray for these two men who were dedicating their lives to preach the gospel, the obvious choice for a leader would be Charlie, a man already proven and accepted by his people.

As I prayed for them, the Lord gave me a word of prophecy concerning them—God had seen Charlie's heart. He would not go to the unreached people, but rather, he would be a pillar in the place where God would plant him. Laying my hands upon John, the most unexpected message came from God—He had chosen John and would send him out to the people of the east and would use him greatly.

As I finished praying for these men, it suddenly hit me. "What have I done?" I wondered. It didn't make any sense. Charlie was the leader, not John.

The incident soon left my mind completely, and in later years this actually came to pass. Charlie settled down and stayed in Inuvik, while much to everyone's amazement, John moved into the east and became the spiritual and natural leader. Again, this supernatural manifestation knit the peoples' hearts to my heart as they realized that these prophecies must be from God.

During those days at Kiklavak when the men were off herding the reindeer or chasing whales, we started the ladies' prayer and Bible-study time. Ten or twelve of us would crowd into Silas's larger tent, the sides flapping loudly in the strong winds while the waves dashed against the rocky shore.

This was a new area of ministry for us all. Eskimo women, like those of many native cultures, have been pushed into the background. The good Eskimo woman is a hard-working wife who is able to look after the skins her husband brings home from the trap line. She keeps busy cleaning the fox pelts, skinning the polar bear and cleaning it. She helps her husband by working with the fish, drying them, and preparing them for storage. She cuts up the big white whale, cooks the muktuk and stores it in the large forty-five-gallon barrels.

Then comes the working of the skins—the task of sewing the fur boots, the fur mitts and parkas to replace the worn-out ones. To the Eskimo, being a dutiful wife means looking after every need, whim and fancy of her husband and family. Yet, somehow, Eskimo women still find time, often daily, to visit each other, drink tea and do the things that women do the world over.

When the gospel of Christ touched the Eskimo, it brought new life to everyone who received it, but especially it added a new dimension of living to Eskimo women. They suddenly realized that their husbands could not take them to heaven, that they could not rely upon their husbands for an understanding of God's Word. They must learn and understand and reach out to God for themselves. For many of them, this opened up a whole new world.

In the ladies' prayer meetings and Bible-study groups, they eagerly became involved in a deeper walk and understanding of the

Lord's ways. We often used flannelgraph illustrations and these they heartily enjoyed. Eskimo people perspire very easily and when they're in deep concentration, beads of sweat literally roll down their faces. Often, as the women would be sitting on the floor in front of me, I would see beads of perspiration merge into streams running down their faces as they sought and struggled to understand.

In those early days, several of them could not read English, but they all had Bibles and they believed that God would help them to read. They applied themselves to study the language, and with God's help, they did learn to read the Word.

The same thing happened with some of the men. I recall one man, Silas, who was wonderfully saved. His whole life was transformed. He had been quite a drunkard and avid gambler, and, consequently, he had many domestic problems. His wife was saved first and witnessed to him until he too gave his life to the Lord. A radical change took place in Silas as he became a "new creature in Christ." He went home and spilled the brew pot out on the snow, as did many other newly-saved Eskimos. And he asked Charlie Smith to make a sign which read, "No More Gambling in This House."

Silas could not read, but each night he knelt by his bed with the open Bible before him and earnestly prayed, "Oh, God, teach me to read your words." Within months Silas could read his English Bible. But if he was given anything else, such as other literature or periodicals, Silas was lost. But he could read and understand the Bible!

I also began Sunday school at Kiklavak Bay and this was always a source of inspiration. Those kids never lacked enthusiasm. How they loved the action choruses such as, "Running Over" and "I Don't Want to Be a Jonah and Be Swallowed by a Whale." They loved to clap their hands as they sang, and they would watch and listen with undivided attention to the flannelgraph presentations.

During this time at Kiklavak Bay, we had been out of touch with the rest of the world for two months and the isolation was beginning to get to me. It's hard to describe the excitement I felt as one day a Cessna 185 circled overhead, then splashed down and taxied up to the beach. Out stepped the manager of Reindeer Station with bags of mail—my first letters from home!

It was so good to hear from my family and Christian friends. I laughed and cried as I read their letters. I read Pastor Layzell's brief letters of counsel, caution and encouragement many times. Mom was fine but wondered how soon I'd be home. It would be three years, but I didn't know that then.

At Kiklavak Bay I was invited to join in my first whale hunt. Eight of us set out on the Moose and after being on the water for approximately an hour, suddenly one of the hunters spotted the beluga whales. What a sight—the beautiful white curve of those elegant creatures arching out of the waves, dipping under, curving up and down, their tails flipping in fluid motion!

Soon the chase was on. As we neared one of the whales, the Eskimo took careful aim with his 303 rifle at the vulnerable area just below its eye. There was a splash and then the whale dived, leaving a stain of red on the surface. They knew he was wounded, so everyone was keenly watching for the whale to come up again. At last we saw him.

As the boat drew close, the Eskimo expertly hurled the harpoon deep into the whale's side. Attached to the harpoon was a floater, usually a ten-gallon drum. Frantically, the whale tried to free himself, swimming in one direction, then in another. Up and down he twisted and swerved, struggling fiercely to live, but his strength was being expended quickly. Red blood stained the water all around him and we knew that the struggle was just about over. Soon the whale would be ours.

Quickly, they circled in closer until they were able to come up behind the whale and kill him with a couple of well-placed shots into the brain. In typical Eskimo custom, one of the Eskimos reached over and sliced off a piece of the flipper, the prize for the victorious hunter. And then we began the task of pulling this two-ton mammoth back to shore.

The men got two whales that day before they joyously made their way back to camp, where the group of smiling women and children eagerly awaited their arrival. Almost as soon as the whale was drawn up on shore, the women went to work on it. This was a big job and took several hours to complete, but it was a happy night in camp for now we had fresh whale meat.

The white meat under the skin is called muktuk. This is carefully cut and partially cooked. Much of the blubber is rendered down; then the semi-cooked muktuk is placed in the blubber and stored for winter in large forty-five-gallon barrels.

During this time I also learned about speedboat travel. The sea near Kiklavak Bay could very quickly blow into a big gale without warning. Often we would be out with the fifteen-foot speedboat when the waves would become choppy and soon the water would be washing over the boat. We'd bail as fast as we could. The Eskimos didn't seem to worry about this. However, one time the water came into the boat so fast that we just couldn't keep up with it, and we very nearly capsized. But again, thanks to the good hand of the Lord upon us, we all made it safely to shore.

One day Mikkel announced that he and Anna and Joseph Pokiak, another herder, were going to make a quick trip to the nearby village of Tuktoyaktuk. I was invited to go along.

As well as stopping at Tuk, we were planning to visit the smaller reindeer camps on the far side of Tuk Bay. The trip would last just one night, and then we would return. But in the Arctic everything is subject to the weather, and the best laid plans of mice and men—or of Eskimos and missionaries. . . .

We anchored our small cabin tugboat in the harbor and went ashore to visit a little lady living in a tent beside the ocean. Teresa and her husband had left the reindeer industry to work on the DEW line, the radar network just being flung across the north at that time. With her five children, Teresa received us very graciously into her little tent. Joseph went off to visit his relatives. We decided that Anna and Mikkel would stay on shore in Teresa's tent. I volunteered to stay in the boat.

The motion of the water didn't prevent me from sleeping, but during the night a violent storm came up. Apparently, the winds had almost taken the tent away, and the reindeer boat was rocking like a hammock.

Fearing that the winds might drag the anchors, Mikkel braved the storm and came out to check in the middle of the night. The storm could continue for several days, so it was only sensible for me to leave the boat and join the others in Teresa's crowded tent.

After five long days and nights, the winds subsided sufficiently for us to go ahead with the trip to the other reindeer herd camp. We arrived there early one afternoon, and not a soul was in sight. Everybody was still sleeping. We found John Maksagak and Helen and a brand new baby. Just a few nights before, Helen had given birth to her first daughter. The nurse had not arrived in time, but the baby and mother were doing fine. Lying in a little reindeer-skin bunting bag was Anna Ruth, a tiny bundle of life the size of a button.

We had a short service in this camp and, not understanding another Eskimo custom, I made a rather stupid mistake. I had decided that I would not take part in the service unless I was asked. But, unknown to me at this time, they had already accepted me as a minister, and therefore automatically expected me to preach. When I did not do so, they were both disappointed and bewildered. This was just one of the many instances of cultural differences which I experienced. It is a constant challenge to a new missionary to be able to understand the customs and social mores of the people to whom they wish to minister.

As we sailed back to Kiklavak Bay, again we passed the village of Tuk, and this bleak and barren little settlement somehow tugged at my heart. Little did I know that in just a year's time, the Lord would permit me to go to that place to establish a mission station.

CHAPTER 6

Winter in a Tent

After my first few months in the Arctic, time started to pass very quickly. No longer did the days lag or the weeks seem unending. In fact, there didn't seem to be enough opportunity to do all the things I wanted to do.

In almost no time, it seemed that the summer months had gone by and we were packing up again—folding the tents, taking the dogs off their lines, again reloading the old scow with everyone's belongings, dogs, children, tents, blankets, and everything else. And so we moved back up the Mackenzie halfway to Reindeer Station.

Kakolak was to be the fall camp, and it was situated right across from one of the new DEW line installations. With astonishment and wonder, the natives of this area had watched the big helicopter descend and land on the hill. The Cat train had moved in and a whole new world of construction was begun out there in the wilderness. The development of the DEW line was the beginning of a new era in the high Arctic.

It was much colder now in late August and September and I had taken up residence in my eight-by-ten-foot tent. Sophie, my young Eskimo friend, had moved in with me, and together we were enjoying tent life. Again, I had much to learn. The little stove which was really a cut-down ten-gallon oil barrel seemed to be always hungry for driftwood. The men had pulled in some drift logs, and then it was each person's responsibility to saw the wood and chop it up for his own tent.

The first few times I used that bucksaw I actually thought my arms would fall off. It felt as if they would be pulled right out of their sockets. But many eyes were watching to see if this frail white woman could cope with the rigors of arctic life, and I was determined to hang in there somehow.

The first stages of freeze-up were upon us, and each morning a thin layer of ice glistened on the water. After a few weeks, the ice was pronounced safe enough to walk on, and we decided to visit the DEW line station. For me it was quite an event to see some other white people. The DEW line personnel were very hospitable, inviting us to a lunch where they spread out their finest—apples and oranges, baked goods, homemade bread, and so many other goodies. The station was still under construction, so the accommodations were rather basic. But compared to ours, theirs seemed almost palatial.

I asked the manager if we could have a service for the boys and invite our Eskimo people to join in, and he obligingly gave us one of the large tents. A number of men came out of curiosity. It struck them as strange that a young white woman would be in this northern wilderness as a minister, and even stranger that I was traveling nomadically with the reindeer herders.

"Why are you here?" they asked. They seemed fascinated that I had come simply because I wanted to serve the Eskimo people with the Christian message.

"We're only here for the dollars," they readily admitted. They knew the hardships, the loneliness and isolation of this land, and to them the idea of anyone choosing to live here indefinitely seemed unbelievable.

During those October days at Kakolak, the hours of daylight became shorter. With winter approaching, living in a tent became more of a challenge. At night the stove would go out completely, and every morning the ice was thicker on the water pail.

It was very difficult to crawl out of the sleeping bag in the mornings now. I soon learned to have the kindling and driftwood all ready the night before. One great advantage of a tent is that it warms up very quickly. After setting a match to the wood, I'd leap back into the sleeping bag for the next few minutes until the tent became liveable again. The increasing cold meant more bucksawing, more splitting wood, more developing of muscles.

After a few weeks we started the move back to Reindeer Station where the children would be in school for the winter months, and the reindeer herders would move into their log houses rather than living in the cold tents. This time we were to travel by dog team.

A sled deer was also harnessed and this was most interesting to watch. With great agility, Mikkel lassoed a deer, and then, very patiently, won the deer's confidence until he was able to put it in harness. When you ride on a sled pulled by a reindeer, hold on, because it takes off with lightning speed. If you're not ready, you'll be left behind.

Because the dog teams could not carry the heavy loads so readily handled by the boat, several trips had to be made to Reindeer Station, some thirty miles south.

Finally the time came for the women and children to be moved. I had my first experience of riding on a toboggan with a dog team. It was much rougher than I expected, because the gale winds blow the snow into high drifts. This causes a constant motion, up and down, bouncing and banging against the washboard type of snow formations. I also discovered that the aroma of the dogs is another unexpected and unpleasant part of dog team travel. One seems to be altogether too close to their tails.

As we bounced over the snowdrifts, the thoughts of Anna's warm cabin appealed greatly to me. By now I didn't view it as just a little cabin with basic living conditions; after the chilling cold and discomfort of the tent, in my mind it seemed almost luxurious. And the constant warmth of an oil heater was perhaps the most appealing thing to me. Anna had great plans for how I would live with them, and it all sounded just heavenly.

At Reindeer Station we began to happily settle into the little log cabins for the winter.

In the middle of all this delightful activity, a message came that I was to go to the station manager's office right away. As I entered Mr. Douglas's office, I was aware that he had something to tell me that he found rather difficult.

"Kayy," he said, "I don't know how to say this, but as you know, Reindeer Station is a federal game preserve. I've just had a reminder from Ottawa that only government-employed people are permitted to live in the log houses on the station." This was devastating news!

"You mean I can't even live with the Pulks in their home?"

"No way, Kayy. I guess you'll just have to pitch a tent for the winter!" he laughingly suggested.

A tent for the winter! I tried to appear unmoved by this sudden turn of events, but as I walked slowly to Anna's house, I fought back bitter tears of disappointment. "Why Lord? Why?" I questioned. Before reaching Anna's house, I tried to regain my composure.

Later that night, as I tossed about in my mind the decision I had to make, to either leave Reindeer Station and perhaps go south, or to accept the challenge of tent life for the whole year, something welled up within me. That call again rang in my heart and in my soul. What a fiery desire to reach these people burned within me! In the quietness of that dark arctic night, my decision was made. I would ask the men if they would help me construct a frame of two-by-fours for my frail tent, and I would stay the winter.

Winter in a Tent

When the Eskimo Christians learned that this white woman would not be moved so easily, that I would stay and live in a tent, they seemed surprised, but pleased.

The next day we began building the tent frame. In the Arctic, material is always hard to come by, but we found a couple of pieces of old plywood to lay on the snow for a floor. As I watched the men pitching my tent, I wondered if there was any chance that I'd ever get rid of the terrible chest cold I'd contracted trying to adjust to this drastically different climate. Fall camp had been especially difficult physically. And now, a winter in a tent in the Arctic? (As it turned out, this heavy cold lasted for my first twelve months.)

We decided to install a small Coleman oil heater in the tent. This eliminated the wood chopping chore. The problem was that the upper part of the tent was kept at a steady warm temperature, but the lower part was extremely cold, usually below freezing.

It didn't take me long to move into the tent with my one suitcase, sleeping bag and a few cooking utensils. An old orange crate for a cupboard, a bunk built of rough boards, a little table that one of the Eskimos had given to me—these were the furnishings of my new home. Sophie was going to sleep with me in the tent, staying at her sister's home in the daytime. Obviously, she could have spent all her time in her sister's warm cabin, but Sophie and others were concerned about me and so she graciously offered to stay part of the time anyway.

In the settlement, a problem arose with another teenage girl who was staying in a home where there were a number of teenage boys. The situation was not good. In order to avoid temptation and the appearance of evil, I suggested that Jean could also sleep with us in the tent. This meant two would sleep on the bunk, but the third person would have to sleep in a sleeping bag on the floor, on a bearskin. I insisted on taking my turn every third night, but when the temperatures on the floor stayed well below minus 35 degrees sometimes I regretted being so noble, so determined to be one of them.

Gradually, we learned how to maneuver in the small area of the tent, even if we couldn't stand up straight except in the very center.

One day I felt inspired to scrub the floor, completely forgetting that there was no insulation beneath the plywood and the temperature outside was 45 degrees below. As quickly as I put the water on the floor it froze, so we ended up with a skating rink. Everyone would literally slide in and out. The ice finally wore away as a result of many mukluks zipping across it. Needless to say, I didn't attempt to wash my floor again that winter.

The darkest days were closing in on us. In November and December, the gas lamp was lit continually, giving off not only good light but extra heat for our little tent. We banked snow blocks up the side walls for additional insulation. Then came the winds of winter, blowing and howling. The tent would flap and flap, and at times it seemed that it would blow away for sure; yet somehow my frail little tent stood.

Once in the middle of the night during a blinding arctic blizzard, I suddenly became aware that something drastic was happening. In the blackness, I felt something wrapping about my head. It was the tent canvas. The ridge pole had broken in the raging winds. Immediately I leaped out of bed to turn off the oil heater, then fumbled around in the darkness to retrieve the ridge pole. But I was helpless. I was alone in the tent, so I climbed into my boots, threw on my parka and trudged over to Anna's house to spend the rest of the night until we could fix the tent.

During this tenting winter, Anna very kindly offered to include my laundry with hers and this I gladly accepted. With no running water and very limited facilities you're lucky to get ice melted for just the basic tasks. With temperatures often at 50 below, it wasn't too conducive to frequent changing of clothes. So on wash day, as I was in Anna and Mikkel's warm cabin, I took the opportunity to change into some nice clean clothes.

At the same time, Mikkel also had the notion to change clothes in their bedroom. As I put on my underwear, I was puzzled to find the crotch hanging down to my knees. I'd never heard of wool that stretches, but this must be it, I figured.

Then I heard Mikkel speaking to his wife in Lappish. This had to be serious talk or he would have used English. Finally it was interpreted. Mikkel couldn't figure out what had happened to his underwear. It had shrunk so he couldn't pull it up past his knees! We discovered the long johns had somehow been switched, and after much giggling, the proper changes were made and life went on.

The weeks and months passed and somehow, living in that tent didn't seem nearly as bad as I had anticipated. Incomprehensible as it may seem, I was almost enjoying it, because I was learning to cope with many new things. The people seemed pleased and rather proud of this little white woman who had done what they had not seen any other white woman do—live in a tent all winter and still be happy. They concluded among themselves that Kayy must really like Eskimos. God must really be with her, or she wouldn't be happy now, they agreed. So out of the circumstance that seemed impossibly difficult, God worked His purpose by causing the people to gain confidence in my ministry among them. As well, it equipped me with vital knowledge and understanding for the pioneer days that would lie ahead.

CHAPTER 7

The Dark Winter Night

During late October, with the increasing darkness, I found it difficult to get up without the sun to announce the day. By mid-November, the sun is a red half-circle squatting briefly on the horizon. Then it becomes just a red glow at noonday, until finally, by the first week of December, there is no evidence of the sun at all. Only a short twilight exists, making it possible for planes to land on the ice between eleven and one o'clock. Gas lamps are on all day long. By two-thirty or three in the afternoon a flashlight is needed to go about the settlement. The long winter night has settled in.

I had wondered how I would cope with the Arctic's long winter night. For most whites, this continual darkness brings on acute despondency and unnatural weariness. Getting up in the dark, working all day with artificial light, going to bed in the dark, brings on fatigue. The white housewives are the hardest hit. They tend to go out less in the dark and cold, and the four walls close in.

During my first winter the darkness was more of a novelty to me.

Yet I remember one winter, years later, after a particularly traumatic period, that the dark season seemed endless and the monotony of it got to me. I couldn't wait for the sun to come up. Soon I learned that activity is the only antidote for darkness.

The long winter night of the high Arctic doesn't have the same effect on the Eskimos, for this is their busiest season. The men are setting their traps and tending the traplines, and the women skin and clean the pelts. Long into the night, every Eskimo woman is working to prepare new boots and parka covers for each member of her household. These must be ready for Christmas, a big event in Eskimo land.

I remember especially the excitement of Christmas mail that first year in the north. Early in December the government bombardier set out across the ice to Aklavik, to pick up our first mail since September. In the darkness of the late afternoon we spotted the bright lights of the bombardier bouncing home across the snowdrifts.

All activity in the settlement came to a halt. Marie, the local postmistress, was preparing supper. Quickly, she pushed the pots to the back of the stove and was waiting in the room that served as post office when the bombardier pulled up and tossed fifteen mail bags onto the kitchen floor. We had to leave Marie alone to sort out this precious mail, so we all congregated in Charlie's house and drank tea and waited. The two hours seemed like two days to me!

Suddenly Charlie's door burst open and a breathless youngster shouted, "The mail is ready!" With that we all zipped up our parkas and dashed for the post office.

I received literally hundreds of Christmas cards, many interesting letters, parcels of home-baked goodies, and thirteen sweaters. I ripped open letter after letter, glanced at the signatures, and then later that night feasted on each one separately. Every letter was such a treat, for they were my only contact with home.

The actual preparations for Christmas got under way in early December. We decided to do a Christmas concert for the community and I had the job of directing the young people and children. They nearly drove me to distraction with their question, "Why do we need rehearsals, Kayy?"

On Christmas morning, we all went from house to house, shaking hands with every man, woman, boy and girl, and exclaiming joyously, "Merry Christmas!" Then there was an open invitation for everyone to squeeze into Charlie's log shack for a Christmas feast. Spread out on the living room floor was a great variety of Eskimo delicacies. It was my first Eskimo smorgasbord, featuring *kuak, mipko* and *oyak* (reindeer meat, raw-frozen, dried and cooked). There was a limited supply of the precious muktuk—the meat of the white whale, semi-cooked and stored in *oksook* (rendered blubber). To me it smelled as if it were fermenting or rotten, but the Eskimos loved it. And six months later, so did I.

There was *akpit,* a special treat of salmonberries collected in jam tins and coffee cans and stored in the ice house (dugouts in the permafrost), *bipsi* and *kuak* (dried and raw-frozen whitefish), all topped off with bannock and jam, tinned butter and gallons of tea.

After this sumptuous dinner, the tin plates and mugs were cleared away, the oilcloth rolled up and William Apsimik grabbed a guitar and began happily strumming lively gospel music.

"I'm So Glad Jesus Lifted Me" and "I've Got Peace Like a River" were some of the favorites. We were all dressed in our new Christmas finery—the Eskimos in their spanking new parka covers and elaborately embroidered *kamiks* (dressy cloth boots with moose hide soles), I in my new jeans and bright red Christmas sweater.

Soon the whole community had crowded in, sitting on the bare board floor, standing around the door—again wall-to-wall Eskimos—and a great service of thanksgiving began.

To the Christian Eskimos, Christmas has special meaning as they sing and testify of God's great love-gift to them, the Lord Jesus Christ. After a great service, we had another cup of tea, bannock and jam, and cake and yeast buns. Around two o'clock we made our way home through the soft drifts of new snow, the northern lights streaking the black sky with a rainbow of light.

The next evening, for a little excitement, we trudged up the high hill behind the settlement, the men pulling the toboggans. We all climbed on the toboggans and started down the hill on a hair-raising ride. We raced around trees, dodging stumps, continuously gathering momentum until, I'm sure, we were hitting fifty miles an hour. I doubted we'd ever reach the bottom. All this by moonlight! Still holding on for dear life, we whizzed through the village and way out onto the river ice.

I quietly heaved a sigh of relief and said, "Thank you, Lord." But the Eskimo young people jumped off eagerly. "Let's do it again!" they shouted. And they did, but this time without me.

CHAPTER 8

Spirit-Filled Eskimos

I had been with the reindeer people now for six months and had been teaching and preaching a great deal about praising the Lord and receiving the experience of the baptism in the Holy Ghost. To my young mind, it seemed very disappointing that since my coming no one had received this baptism although many had become a little more free in praise and worship.

I was almost in despair over this situation, but God had a surprise in store for all of us. After again ministering on the subject of the Holy Spirit, an unusual thing happened. Danny Sidney, perhaps the most shy and retiring man of the group, suddenly knelt down for prayer and tearfully said, ''I want to receive this experience from God.''

The brethren gathered around him and we just simply prayed for him. Suddenly Danny lifted his hands heavenward and began to praise and worship God from the depths of his being. After only a moment or two, he began to speak in other tongues and was wonderfully baptized in the Holy Ghost. We left the meeting rejoicing in what God had done.

At the service next evening an evident change had taken place in Danny. No longer too shy to open his mouth, he was the first one to testify, and with new impetus and power began to open God's Word and exhort like a man from another world. I didn't get a chance to preach that night; Danny took over. This change in Danny inspired faith and created a fresh desire in the other believers' hearts to receive more from God too.

Joseph Pokiak had been out with the herd and so had missed the service when Danny received this wonderful experience. But Joseph was in the meeting Sunday morning when we gathered for prayer, and then for the morning service.

We began to sing, "Wonderful, Wonderful Jesus," worshiping and praising our lovely Lord. Without any prompting, Joseph began to speak forth in a melodious language of other tongues. Sitting on the floor during the song service, he was wonderfully baptized in the Holy Ghost.

This was just the beginning. A little later on in another service, Laura Kanegana became aware of God's presence strongly upon her. Sitting on the floor without anyone praying for her—her heart reaching out to God—Laura suddenly jumped up and burst forth in tongues. Then she did something that she didn't even know was in the Bible as a form of worship—Laura began to dance before the Lord. Later she was worried that she'd done something wrong, but when she saw Psalm 149:3, "Let them praise his name in the dance. . . ."—Laura was delighted and relieved.

In the afternoon ladies' prayer meeting, we studied God's Word together, and then began to take individual requests. Laura Pokiak asked if all the women would pray for her, that she might receive more from God to strengthen her in her life. She was a little Eskimo woman, perhaps twenty-two years of age, who already had borne five children. Her life was hard, but she wanted to truly serve the Lord.

We gathered around her and prayed that God would meet her

heart's desire, and there in that little log shack, the Holy Ghost visited again and Laura was filled with an overflowing joy.

She received a very unusual experience, one I had not seen before nor since. Laura's heart was so full that this heavenly language kept bursting from her. For several days as she went about praying with her friends, even just going about her household duties, Laura's cup of new wine was constantly spilling over. She was absolutely basking in the glory of this experience with a glow about her that was a most effective witness for Christ. All fear and shyness was gone from her heart. Laura exhorted the young people and stirred them to serve God. We didn't realize it at that time, but God was granting her a little bit of glory to go to heaven with, for in just two short years, Laura passed away. Her death was the result of an ectopic pregnancy and she entered into the fullness of the presence of the Lord.

That afternoon when Laura received the Holy Spirit, Anna Pulk left the ladies' prayer meeting very discouraged. She concluded that God had forgotten her, that He loved others more, that she was not worthy to receive the gift of the Holy Ghost herself.

Anna hardly ever hit a spiritual low, but this day she did. To Mikkel she said in her Lappish tongue, "Why does everyone receive this except me? Why won't God give it to me? There's no use for me to pray anymore." Mikkel could only tell her that it was God's gift, that she would have to talk to God about it.

That evening, as we had devotions together in the home, Anna was weeping, pouring her heart out to the Lord. After a little time of prayer, Anna raised her hands and instead of crying, she began praising God, thanking and worshiping Him.

This sudden burst of worship and adoration continued for about a half hour and then another strange thing happened to Anna. She leaned backwards at about a 35-degree angle and stayed in this position. She remained like this not just for a few seconds, but for ten or fifteen minutes. We knew that God was doing something special for Anna, so we waited in the Lord's presence, quietly worshiping and praising Him and letting Him minister to this woman who loved Him so very much.

After some time had passed, Anna began to clap her hands and suddenly she burst forth in an unknown tongue, a heavenly language, her spirit communing with God. Oh, the joy she knew as she received a remarkable experience, being baptized in the Holy Ghost!

After about an hour in the Lord's presence, Anna suddenly got up and embraced us. "Kayy," she said, "I want to go over and pray with Laura who received the Holy Ghost today." So about one in the morning, we pulled on our parkas and ran over to Laura's little cabin. As we opened the door, there was Laura on the reindeer skin on the floor, praying, praising God and speaking in tongues. Anna joined her on the reindeer skin, and together they began to praise God in other tongues.

The little generator that supplied electricity to the cabins at Reindeer Station was turned off every morning at 1:45. I figured when the lights went off, this little prayer meeting would come to an end and we'd all go home to bed. At 1:45 the lights did flicker and go out. I wasn't quite so caught up in this heavenly visitation, and quickly scrounged around the house looking for a candle. None of this commotion stirred Anna and Laura. They just kept on praying, perhaps for another half hour.

Finally, Anna arose, and we went out in the winter night. The moon was shining brightly, the snow was crunching under our feet. There was a lightness about Anna's movement that night, for she had received an experience with God that she would never forget.

I supposed that when we got back to Anna's cabin, we would just go to bed. But Anna had another suggestion. "Let's have another short prayer together," she enthused. The short prayer extended for two hours; we finally went to bed at about five o'clock. I dropped off to sleep, hearing beautiful words coming from Anna's room. "Thank you, Jesus. Oh, thank you, Jesus!" she repeated over and over again.

The next day Anna was still overflowing with the presence of God, so I suggested to her that I would do the housework while she visited the women of the station. Happily, Anna joined Laura and they went from house to house rejoicing in God's goodness, praying with everyone. The little Christian community was amazed at the goodness of God to His people.

And that's how it was when God moved in sovereignly by His Spirit. Many more received wonderful experiences from the Lord. Many were endued with new power and new strength from on high. The Word of God became more alive and wonderful to them, as the inspiration of God's Spirit gave them understanding.

Soon the word reached nearby communities that God was moving by His Spirit at Reindeer Station. Some of the Christians from Aklavik and Inuvik came to the station that they too might be blessed, filled and refreshed in God. Many of those who received from the Lord and were filled with His Holy Spirit, later testified that this experience and the reality of the presence of God held them through many a storm along life's journey and equipped them to witness and stand true for God.

Also during those days and months at Reindeer Station, on different occasions, God gave me a word of prophecy concerning these people: "That God would scatter them, and that these were their days to be strengthened and ministered to and equipped for the days when they would have to stand alone."

It seemed a strange prophecy, and yet it burned like a fire within me. A few years later, a very surprising turn of events happened as the reindeer industry was turned over to private hands (to Silas, one of our Eskimo Christian herders) and the government station was abandoned. The reindeer herders moved to various settlements seeking employment. Indeed they were "scattered abroad," but those days at Reindeer Station when God was pouring out His Spirit, became the strength and stability of their lives. Flying today over the totally desolate Reindeer Station is mute testimony that God watches over His word to bring it to pass.

CHAPTER 9

Journey by Dog Team

During the spring months, before the ice and snow had gone, I decided to venture on my first long dog team trip. The sun was now back many hours of the day and long into the evening, making it an ideal time for such travel. Nels loaned us his dogs and Sophie agreed to come along.

It was a lot of fun getting ready, with Anna insisting on numerous extra supplies as safeguards in case we were unexpectedly delayed along the trail. Finally, all was lashed on the sled, the dogs were harnessed, and we took off for Aklavik some sixty miles away. Because the spring sun softens the snow, making the pulling much heavier for the dogs, the custom is to sleep during the day and wait for evening when the snow hardens.

We jogged along for several hours and then camped with an old Eskimo couple in their little shack on the shores of the delta. It was muskrat season, so we sat down to roast muskrat. The meat was good, but the sight of the long muskrat tails bothered my stomach considerably.

After supper we watched the tedious process of skinning these small animals so their fur pelts are not torn. With infinite patience, the old Eskimo woman sat on the floor working hour after hour, carefully skinning the muskrats.

Next day we pushed on for Aklavik. We arrived at noon, surprising Ellen Binder who was cooking caribou stew on her one burner oil range. She was so attractive and glowing, with her beautiful brown eyes, her lustrous dark hair tied back with bright wool. We had hardly entered her home when her four children burst in from school, dirty and wet from slipping and sliding along the muddy wooden sidewalks of the settlement. I've never seen anything like the mud in Aklavik in springtime. In the gutters small rivers of melted snow float along all the debris of the winter's garbage—cigarette boxes, candy bar papers, pop and beer bottles.

Otto, a special constable with the Royal Canadian Mounted Police, tethered our dogs down along the river near his dogs, feeding them their ration of one twelve-inch fish each. The dogs create quite a commotion by yapping and snarling when they know it's feeding time. They gulp the fish down, then curl up in a ball in the snow, noses under their tails, and are soon fast asleep.

We planned to rest the dogs a day or two, then return home, but Charlie Gordon, the Eskimo church leader, invited me to stay and have services with them on Sunday. I hadn't planned on this and had come to town with no dress clothes. So on Saturday I went to the Hudson's Bay store to find something suitable for preaching. But I had no luck. "Well, Lord, you'll have to bless me as I am, jeans and plaid shirt."

A few minutes before eight o'clock on Sunday night, we slid through the mud to the dilapidated hotel where the services were being held. Plywood scraps were nailed over some of the broken windows. The door was bowed and grubby. Inside the paint had been worn off the floor; the counter of the cafe, once bright red, was now scratched and dirty. A dozen Eskimo and Indian young people slouched on stools around the counter, with an old record player blaring. A few older men, obviously intoxicated, stopped their loud talk to watch curiously as we walked past them into the hall that had been partitioned off for the movie theater. The backless benches were splintered and rickety, badly in need of repair. The floor had not been washed, not even swept, and debris had just been pushed to the sides. It was a dark, dingy room lit by a few bare 100-watt bulbs dangling from the ceiling.

Charlie took his place at the front, leading the Eskimos in a rousing sing-song with his fine bass voice. Charlie was Alaskan-born, a massive man in his early fifties, with beautiful, thick, wavy black hair which was greying slightly. He always had a happy expression, an exuberance born of inward joy. With his wife, Thea, he was given to hospitality.

How I loved Thea, this tiny Eskimo lady still exceptionally beautiful at fifty, with her jet-black hair pinned back in an attractive roll. She was an outstanding seamstress, sewing muskrat parkas with Alaska-style trim, embroidered *kamiks* and fur-trimmed mukluks. Thea was wearing her parka over a crisp print dress; Charlie had on a colored shirt and khaki pants tucked into his mukluks.

My sermon title was, "Prepare to Meet Thy God." The next door cafe became very quiet as I began to preach, and later I learned that its patrons were a part of my audience. God was very gracious in that eight or nine people came forward for salvation.

The next day we started for home, and had a wonderful trip. We traveled all morning and most of the afternoon, even though it was a little hard pulling. The sun was shining brightly now—a beautiful opportunity to get an arctic tan. In springtime the Eskimos become very dark (they describe themselves as black). Even with my fair skin, I was able to pick up quite a windburn and tan that day. Sophie and I had a delightful time, taking turns riding in the sled and driving the dogs, laughing and joking together. We arrived back at the station in time for a tasty reindeer steak at Sophie's sister's house.

However, those happy days in Reindeer Station were not without problems. As we ministered God's Word and the Holy Spirit was poured out, a difficulty arose between Brother Charlie and me. The enemy uses any means to bring disunity; in this instance it was a misunderstanding.

As I look back on it now, I wonder if perhaps Charlie was feeling insecure since I had come among them to minister. He had faithfully earned the position of spiritual leader. Was a young, inexperienced white girl going to rob him of this? I'm sure I could have handled the situation more wisely if only I had been a little more mature.

A molehill of difficulty soon became mountainous. Charlie no longer came to the meetings and he would not discuss the problem. This caused me great concern but as I put the problem before the Lord, I felt I just had to leave it in God's hands and let Him work it out. This posed a real problem, because we met for services in Charlie's house. Would the Eskimo people stand behind me if we met somewhere else?

The teacher gave us the use of the school, and very falteringly I called a service. All of the Eskimo people came as usual, except Charlie. I shared with the people how sorry I felt that this had happened, but that we must recognize it as the work of the enemy and continue to pray until the breach was healed.

About this time another trial came upon us. Measles hit Reindeer Station. Because it was spring break-up, it was impossible for a plane to land, or a boat to move toward the hospital in Aklavik. We were cut off, totally isolated from help. It was a severe measle epidemic. Home after home was affected, children and adults alike. The manager at the station asked if I would assist in looking after these people. I told him I would.

For the next three weeks I spent my time ministering to the people's physical needs. One woman, Laura, and her teenage daughter were dreadfully ill. They couldn't be left alone day or night, so I took the night shift, praying that God would spare their lives. For a few nights Laura was in a state of delirium. Both of their temperatures were raging to 105 degrees. Not knowing what else to do, I bathed them to bring their temperature down, and gave them regular antibiotic injections. For several nights they hovered between life and death. Often, as I was wearily finishing my shift and preparing to leave, Janette would say, "Please, Kayy, can I have another bath?" Finally, I'd get home by late morning and tumble into bed; then in a few hours, someone else would need help.

After two or three weeks I was so tired that I couldn't eat, and often I couldn't sleep. The concern over Charlie's problem always weighed heavily on me, as did the serious condition of the very sick. But in those days I learned to cast my care on Him, for He truly cares for us (1 Pet. 5:7).

By the time the doctor arrived, the critical period was over and all were on the mend. He was amazed that we had not lost a single patient. How we thanked God!

The Charlie problem had gone on now for over a month. How we longed to see everything brought back into unity. A mediator was needed, someone Charlie would respect and relate to. Just then the familiar sound of a small aircraft zoomed overhead—Don Violette's plane! God's answer was flying in.

That evening, Don invited Charlie to a service in the school, and he came.

"The Bible says if your brother has aught against you, then go to your brother," Don was saying.

Was this the way? I certainly wanted this conflict resolved, so I got to my feet and went over to Charlie.

"Charlie," I pled, "I'm sorry for this problem, but I want you to know I have nothing in my heart against you." Charlie broke and wept and wept. He asked my forgiveness, everyone else's forgiveness, and told how lonely he had been without Christian fellowship. That day the breach was healed, and a deep bond of friendship was born in Charlie's heart and mine. We became very good friends; never again did we have a difficulty. Everybody rejoiced, and a new step was taken in the learning process of walking with God and our fellow believers.

His mission of reconciliation completed, Don had to leave very quickly because of shifting ice conditions. He had arrived just after the initial ice break-up when the ice begins to lift, and the water runs off. Don had made one of his famous three point landings. One time, an R.C.M.P. officer had observed Don coming in on a very short strip of ice, making a perfect landing. Said the Mountie. "When I get religion, I want the kind that guy's got!"

Pioneering with the Gospel

CHAPTER 10

Tuk

In just a few days the ice would break up completely and drift down the Mackenzie to the sea. Already I had cast my eyes on the village of Tuktoyaktuk, a bleak settlement with perhaps three hundred Eskimos huddling in shacks on the barrens along the Arctic Ocean, about ninety miles northeast of Reindeer Station. I knew it would be a very difficult village to penetrate with the gospel, but I planned to move there just as soon as river travel was possible.

Sophie had decided to come with me, so in early July when all the ice had gone out, we were able to hitch a ride with one of the herders, Wallace Lucas. We loaded our few belongings, including our trusty tent, into his twenty-two-foot freighter canoe with outboard motor and headed off down the beautiful MacKenzie.

Once we reached the Beaufort Sea, the waves began rocking us, splashing over the sides of our canoe till we were all soaked to the skin. Even though I had on a leather jacket and wore long johns under my jeans, the cold wind whipping across the ocean soon chilled me to the bone. We had wrapped most of our things in the tarpaulin of our tent, but even so, they were drenched with the spray. After ninety cold, choppy, dousing-wet miles, we rounded the narrow rocky spit and headed into the harbor of Tuktoyaktuk.

Log shacks were scattered along the curve of the shore. Dogs yapped at their stakes on the beach. The spires of the white frame Catholic church and the log Anglican sanctuary rose above the little homes. There was the small white and blue mounted police detachment with the Union Jack flying overhead. The white, plywood, one-room school was noticeable also. We passed the dock of the Hudson's Bay Company where a dozen or so Eskimos were sitting on the steps wearing print parka covers to ward off the mosquitoes.

I had visited Tuk for a few hours once during the previous winter, in an endeavor to secure a building site. As we had stepped off the plane that day in March, the blustery winds so common on the coast were blowing across the ice and it was bitterly cold. Darkness was fast closing in, and the pilot was anxious to have the business accomplished and get out of there before the weather changed.

The R.C.M.P. officer and I had trudged across the crunchy snow to stake a claim in unsurveyed territory. The snow was three or four feet deep and the whole area was blanketed by high snow drifts, but we chose a spot at the base of the pingo and I dashed back to the plane and the impatient pilot.

This day in July as Sophie and I pushed the canoe ashore, that staked property looked quite different. It was a poor piece of land, boggy and totally unsuitable for a building site. But this is what had been allotted to us, so this we would use.

With Wallace's help we set up the tent and put our belongings in it; then we set up a smaller tent beside it to house the supplies that we hoped were coming—materials to build a house, plus winter food and fuel.

When I had written from Reindeer Station to my home church in

Vancouver, telling them of my burden to move to Tuk, they responded quickly, pledging their support for building materials and necessary supplies to launch the work. This was only the first of many such instances of truly sacrificial giving, often double tithing, when the congregation at Glad Tidings Temple rallied to the support of arctic missions, even though their mission budget was already strained to the limit.

My first night in Tuk, walking around the dirt trails of the settlement, a whole new world of anticipation gripped me as I set my hand to pioneer with the gospel of Jesus Christ. On the whole, the people were quite friendly, but yet a little uncertain and perhaps a little skeptical about my move to Tuk. By now, several of them had been warned against us and our teaching, so there were some barriers behind the smiles.

While we were waiting for the supply ship, we plastered ourselves with bug lotion each day, and, fighting off the mosquitoes, set out to meet the people. Gradually these people became very dear friends, especially one old Christian couple, Ed and Violet Kikoak, who had been saved for about two years.

Despite the mocking and scoffing of their many relatives and friends, they had held on to their new-found faith. Violet was very mother-like to me, always looking after clothes that needed a stitch and often inviting me to eat with them.

Brother Ed had been disabled by a stroke, yet he never missed a service. He was quite a heavy man and found it difficult to walk over the hill with his stick, dragging one leg. Nonetheless, he would be there faithfully, good weather or bad, blowing winds or howling storm. To Ed, it made no difference; he would always be in church with Violet.

One morning Sophie poked her head out of the tent to see what kind of a day it was, and there in the harbor was a welcome sight. The freighter had come during the night, bringing with it two or three barges. Surely our supplies would be on board. Quickly we made a cup of tea and hurried over to the dock.

The purser wasn't available, so I went on board looking for the captain. When I found him he said, "We have material and foodstuffs for a Rev. Kayy Gordon. Don't tell me that's you!" He was taken aback. "I wasn't expecting a woman to be pioneering up here.

"All right, Kayy, where do you want the stuff put?" he asked.

That was a good question. This was a problem I had been tossing about in my mind for weeks. All those two-by-fours and plywood, the insulation and sheeting, plus a year's supply of food and fuel oil—how would Sophie and I transport it to our building site three quarters of a mile from the dock? The captain saw our dilemma and very helpfully ordered the forklift operator to drop all our supplies on the doorstep. How I thanked the Lord for this kindness!

This first summer in Tuk, as we began to open the boxes from the boat, we felt as if Christmas had come early. Part of the food order had not arrived, but we did have instant potatoes, canned ham, canned peas, and two cases of apple-lime juice. There was a large parcel of woolen sweaters, socks, and beautiful things from the Glad Tidings ladies' missionary band. Sophie was especially fascinated with a uniquely designed soup ladle. We had a great time together, unpacking all the goodies and then trying to find a place to put them.

As for the building materials, I knew above everything else that we had to keep the insulation dry. First of all, we stashed it away in our little storage tent. To our dismay, the insulation filled the whole tent! What could we do with all the food stuffs and household items? They'd just have to fit into the back of our little sleeping tent, as if we weren't crowded enough!

Our one piece of furniture—an inexpensive couch—arrived. This also had to go into the tent, because we couldn't leave it outside in the dampness. Yet I was delighted that it had come on the first boat, because we were having an extra-special treat that summer. My friend, Dorothy Williams, was coming to visit me for a month. I seized the chance to go to Aklavik to meet her, and as the plane touched down on the smooth waters of Aklavik with Dorothy on board, I remember thinking, "Isn't it great! We now have everything we need. We have food, a couch to sleep on, and things will be just so much better," not realizing that we still were living very meagerly. It was a great joy to see Dorothy after one year away from home. There seemed so much to talk about, so much to share.

The next day we climbed aboard Don Violette's little Cessna 185 for our flight to Tuk. As we were taking off, I mentioned to Don that I'd never had an exciting ride in a small plane. "Oh, I see!" Don smiled. The weather was perfect and the wind conditions were just right, so Don did a few tricks with his plane that delighted me, but not Dorothy. "How am I ever going to get back?" she asked in dismay. "I'll never fly in a little plane again!"

We landed at Tuk and I was so happy to take her to our little abode. When she saw our small tent on the tundra, jammed to the ridge pole with lumber and packing boxes, I suppose her reaction was a very normal one. She simply said, "Good night, Kayy. Are you trying to live in *this*?" A little later on she asked where the washroom was. "Just go over the hill, and if anybody's around they'll look the other way," was my answer.

Coming from the city, she found our style of tent life quite a challenge. One day we were squatting on the ground, cooking bannock, when the tent flap opened. A very proper school teacher who delighted in serving tea in fine bone china cups was standing there. She was very gracious, but Dorothy was mortified.

A few nights after her arrival, a terrible wind blew up. Dorothy was sleeping on the new couch and I was in my sleeping bag on the floor. I'm a sound sleeper, and by then I was accustomed to high winds so I didn't even awaken during the storm. But Dorothy did.

"Wake up, Kayy!" she cried. "We're going to be blown into the ocean!"

"It'll be all right, Dot. Just go back to sleep," I mumbled, turning over and going back to sleep.

Poor Dorothy was in a dilemma. The rain was beating in through the flap of the tent. The inexpensive, wine-colored couch was soon soaked and bleeding all over Dorothy's nightgown. Again she called me, but still no response. Finally a great gust of wind blew in and the ridge pole collapsed. Down came the tent on top of us. This was enough to awaken even me, and reluctantly I crawled out of my warm sleeping bag, which also had become damp in places, and proceeded to replace the fallen ridge pole. It was hopeless to try to sleep after that.

Of course it was daylight all night anyway, so we decided we might just as well get up. With the primus stove pumped and lit, soon the tent began to feel warm, and we enjoyed a simple cup of hot tea that early morning. It was a dull, grey day so there was little hope of drying out the wet tent. We just had to stay in the damp tent that day, hoping for better weather the next day. Even I didn't sleep too well that night.

The next day did bring better things. The sun was shining brightly, the wind had dropped and the rain had subsided. We began the task of taking everything out of the tent and putting it in the bright sunshine, hoping it would dry. Then we began to prepare the meal: instant mashed potatoes, canned ham, canned peas, apple-lime juice and tea. The next meal was the same, and the next, and the next. During the whole month of Dorothy's visit, that was the extent of our cuisine. Occasionally the Eskimos would bring us fresh fish. After that steady fish diet at Kiklavak Bay the previous summer, fish was not especially my favorite food, but at this point it seemed like steak.

Another very real problem that summer was the drinking water. During the winter the men would cut ice blocks from a close-by fresh-water lake. But in summer there's no transportation across the tundra, so this meant they had to go by canoe around the bay, up an inlet to a fresh-water lake, dip with pails till they had filled a couple of forty-five-gallon drums, and then return—an hour and a half's chore. This was an impossibility for us because we had no canoe. However, Sophie prevailed upon some of the Eskimo men to bring water for us. Still we had to conserve our drinking water very carefully.

One time the wind blew relentlessly for four or five days. Our water supply, like that of most of our neighbors, was depleted. Yet no one could get across to the lake because of the storm and high winds. There was only one thing to do—drink apple-lime juice. At one stage we had to use it to rinse off our dishes and wash our faces, but it didn't make very good tea. After a couple of weeks, Dorothy said to me one morning, "Kayy, have you ever felt called to Africa?"

CHAPTER 11

The Church on the Tundra

Somehow in the midst of entertaining my guest I had to get on with the task of building a house, but I hadn't a clue as to where I could begin. And right then, a young Christian man from the Northern Transportation Company arrived.

"Can you tell us where to start on this pile of lumber?" we asked him.

He had done some carpentry so he pitched in and started the framing and laying the floor; and then suddenly he was called to another base.

"To build this house is a man's job!" he protested. "Surely God is not asking you two girls to put up a house!"

Well, there's real women's lib in the Arctic. The women work right alongside the men, and just as hard. So I guessed as Christian women, we had to share in this difficult role.

It was almost time for Dorothy to leave, and inwardly I was dreading it. The pangs of loneliness were beginning to bite and sting, and I was frustrated at not knowing how to get the house up.

Everything seemed to be going haywire. I wasn't kidding myself. Circumstances were far from rosy.

On the last day of Dorothy's arctic visit, I flew as far as Aklavik with her, and then stood alone on the shore, watching the little Otter taxi out over the choppy waves, then lift off, carrying away Dorothy and all she represented of my ties with home and loved ones. Flying back to Tuk, my heart was so very heavy. Returning to the little tent was especially lonely, for Sophie was away visiting relatives for a few days and I was completely alone.

The blanket that Dorothy had used was folded in the corner. I went over to pick it up, and there was a nest of mice! This was all I needed. If there's one thing on this earth I can't stand, it's baby mice with no hair on their scrawny bodies, no hair on their long tails. Suddenly I was overcome with nausea, and dashed outside. After throwing up, I returned to the tent, purposefully picked up the blanket—the nest, the baby mice, the whole mess—walked down to the shore and tossed it all into the ocean.

I went back to my tent, and for the first time since coming to the Arctic, I broke down and began to cry uncontrollably. "Why, God, does it have to be this way? Why does everything have to go wrong? Why does it have to be so hard?" How I wished I had gotten on that plane with Dorothy to fly south and forget the whole thing. I had hit the pit of despair and I knew it.

With great effort, I brushed away the tears and told myself, "This is weakness. You've got to be strong." Very unenthusiastically I tried to prepare a meal of mashed potatoes, canned ham, and canned peas. But I pushed it away, unable to eat. I had no source of distraction, no radio, no tape recorder, no record player, nothing. I opened the hymnbook and tried to sing a few lines, but my voice would trail off, so I would try another song. Finally I closed the hymnal, stood to my feet, and from the depths of my being cried, "Oh, God, give me grace and guts!"

"This is ridiculous," I thought. "I'm a lot bigger than those horrid baby mice''—and the thought made me laugh at myself. "I can't stay in this tent and brood. I'll dress up and go out and visit."

After a quick wash-up in about a cup of water, I put on my favorite slacks and a brand new sweater and took a little stroll along the shoreline until I was sure no traces of my upset remained. Then I proceeded to visit the native homes, and this proved to be an encouragement.

Sharing in the problems of these people and encouraging them has lifted me many times since then. They are so warm, so hospitable. They have such a simple way of receiving visitors. After a few hours I returned to my tent singing, with a new confidence and a new trust in God. I looked over at that pile of lumber, and felt a challenge in my soul. "Oh, God, as you strengthened Nehemiah of old, so strengthen my hands to rise and build," I cried aloud.

When Sophie returned, we had to figure out a course of action. Some new government buildings were going up across town, so each day we'd slip over and study their construction, then hurry back to try it on our building project. It looked so easy for those carpenters, but somehow we couldn't get the boards to run straight, and when we tried to drive three-inch spikes into fir two-by-sixes we seemed to spend more time trying to take out one bent nail than it would have taken to drive in ten more spikes.

Gradually we learned how to handle the square and level, and things began to fit together. We worked long hours, our arms aching from sawing timbers and driving nails. Finally the little house was nearly enclosed. But how do we handle the windows and doors? I was completely buffaloed.

Sophie had an idea. She knew an old Eskimo man who would be able to fit the doors and windows for us. Amos came over, but he had never seen a window sash. He only knew how to put in a single fixed pane, so he trimmed away most of the sashes and fitted the windows in place. So what if they couldn't be opened? For us they filled the gap and we were happy.

It had become apparent that we couldn't leave the house in this low-lying boggy area. But where should it go, and how could we get it there? We decided on a satisfactory location and claimed squatters' rights. With the help of the DEW-line personnel along with their two big Cats, within an hour our house was sitting on its new site, high and dry.

With the increasing chill of winter, we hurried to finish off the interior. Finally, by the end of October, it was completed. To Sophie and me, this fourteen-by-twenty-foot roughly hewn building seemed like a palace. It was so spacious after the eight-by-ten-foot tent that we had lived in for the previous sixteen months.

We had been holding services in the house of Edward Kikoak, one of the first Christians in Tuk, but now everyone wanted to crowd into our place. So we had to make a choice—would we have furniture or people? There was really no choice. Wall-to-wall people beats tables and chairs any day.

We built benches around three walls, and partitioned off a tiny sleeping corner with two makeshift bunks for our reindeer skins and sleeping bags, plus another two-by-three-foot corner of the "honey bucket." The primus stove sat on an orange crate and gas lamps hung from the ceiling.

We spread a piece of oilcloth on the floor and ate Eskimo-style, praying the Lord to bless this house. Our prayers were answered because the joy of the Lord came down again and again in that plain, little house as Eskimo families turned to Christ.

The night of our first service will always stand out in my memory. The ice on the bay was a foot thick. It was an extremely cold night with much blowing snow. But in spite of the cold, to my great delight, towards eight o'clock, the people began to gather from all across the settlement. Mothers came with babies in their *attigi* (parkas), and fathers carried toddlers on their shoulders. They stopped on our little porch to beat the snow out of their fur parkas. We'd driven a few spikes high up on the walls, but not enough to hold all the parkas. Soon thirty to forty Eskimos were jammed into that little area. They filled the benches and then sat on every inch of the floor. What a joy it was to begin to teach them the gospel of Jesus Christ.

The space heater (turned off, of course) served as a pulpit. For an altar we cleared a little space up front where people could kneel to make a public commitment of their lives to Jesus Christ. After the service, we would roll out the oilcloth and have some tea and homemade bannock or donuts and a time of fellowship together. Without an oven we could not bake cakes, but we soon learned to whip up eight dozen yeast donuts in a big cast-iron frying pan on the primus stove. Dipped in sugar, these were favorites with the Eskimos.

Tuk people came freely to the services. They listened politely, but there was no obvious response. After a few weeks, while walking home across the ice from visiting a family some two miles away, Sophie turned to me with puzzled concern. "Kayy, why aren't the people getting saved?" Little did she know that that was the big question in my mind also.

I was great on the "Why Lords?" I know now I had to learn to sow much seed, to sow in faith and to plow in faith, and in God's time the harvest would come. But it seemed to be such a long growing period. Sometimes despair would almost sweep over me. I tried to keep these things to myself, for I knew Sophie was discouraged too. What good would it do if she knew how I really felt?

At this same time, I was going through a stage of feeling very inferior to everyone. By "moccasin telegraph" I had heard that most of the other whites in town resented my being there. I was being criticized for over-identifying with the natives. Certainly, my living quarters were poor in comparison with the homes of other white people. I felt severely ostracized, very much a second-class minority citizen.

In these times of testing, I learned to lift my eyes to the Lord. How grateful I was that Pastor Layzell had instilled into us the sound teaching that the just shall live by faith and not by feelings; that no matter how we *felt*, we should rise in *faith*, give thanks to God and bless His name, and see the victory come.

However the whites must have felt about me, I certainly never lacked for Eskimo visitors; in fact, my house in Tuk was like Grand Central Station with people coming and going at any hour of the day or night. My door was never locked and I remember coming home from a late afternoon of visiting to find the gas lamp lit and someone playing my guitar. It was Bessie, a young Roman Catholic Eskimo who just loved to sing and play. Although she came often to services, in all my time at Tuk, Bessie never made a stand for the Lord. But twelve years later, this same Bessie gave her heart to Jesus Christ in the Tuk church. Those early days of befriending her and witnessing to her were as seed sown that in God's time brought forth fruit unto salvation. Our God is so faithful.

Another time a strange smell greeted me as I opened the door. During my absence someone had turned on the primus stove, and bubbling away was a polar bear stew. My good next-door neighbor, Mona, had brought it over for me. As soon as my lamp was lit, Mona came in all smiles, and she had her little boy with her. "Little Johnny so touchy," she explained to me. I looked at little Johnny, expecting to see him very nervous. But instead, I saw him grabbing things, picking up everything. "See what I mean? He always so touchy."

Our English language provided many opportunities for humorous misunderstandings. Once when one of the young Christians was all fired up as he was testifying in a service, he turned to Daniel's story of Belshazzar and the handwriting on the wall: "Thou art weighed in the balances and art found wanting" (Dan. 5:27). "That's the way it is with us Eskimo," Billy concluded. "God weighs us in His balance and He finds us wanting—wanting a snowmobile, wanting new clothes, wanting a new house. . . ." He was really preaching away, and I could hardly keep from cracking up.

CHAPTER 12

The Reindeer Camp

One afternoon there was a timid knock at my door and there stood a white woman—Iona Blakney, the new nurse in town. She wouldn't come in; she had just dropped by to say hello. I had heard that Iona was an exceptionally good nurse but quite a party girl; in fact, they said, she could drink any man under the table. I was surprised to have her call. She was the first white woman to do so.

Iona asked me to drop by the nursing station, and there she presented me with a gift of fresh meat and chicken. There was something so very kind and gracious about this unsaved woman. I wished I could get to know her better.

Early in January, while visiting patients in the nursing station, I mentioned to Iona that I would like to make a trip to a reindeer camp fifty miles away, a day's travel by dog team.

"I'd love to go with you, Kayy," Iona exclaimed. I was floored on two counts: first that she would consider a trip like that. Most white women don't leave the warmth and comfort of their homes during the cold arctic winter. And second, I was amazed that Iona would want to go with me, since I was a bit of an outcast in the eyes of the other whites in town. But the voice inside said, "Take her, Kayy." Together we laid plans.

Two weeks later I borrowed a team of dogs from Peter, one of the Christian men. Nels had come to Tuk for a visit and he would drive his team and act as guide. As well, in our party we would have two Eskimo men who were traveling to the Husky Lakes area. Iona would be doing some immunization and she would conduct a baby clinic; I hoped to minister to the herders for a couple of days.

We had to plan carefully for this winter trek across the barren lands, taking enough food—lots of hardtack (very hard pilot biscuits), sardines, (they don't freeze easily) pork and beans, spaghetti, and lots of tea and bannock. Although bannock freezes, it quickly thaws when dunked in tea.

We needed the proper clothing—fur parkas, fur pants, fur boots, fur mitts—and with all that on, we could hardly move. Finally all was ready, and we pulled out of Tuk about nine in the morning on one of the worst days of the winter—cold and overcast.

Normally our trip would take eight hours, but fresh snow had fallen, making it extremely difficult for the dogs. In an effort to lighten the load, we took turns running beside the toboggan. Iona was a lot of fun and the hours passed quickly.

But Iona was having a problem. She was a chain smoker, and at one point her cigarette went out before she could light another one. The wind was blowing so strongly that lighting her cigarette became a major operation. Finally, with Iona on her knees and her face almost to the ground and me huddling over her with my arms spread out for a windbreak, after about twenty minutes Iona got a light.

But we had fallen far behind our guide who fortunately had noticed our lagging and had stopped to wait. Need I say I got a severe reprimand for such a foolish delay? Yet it was this strange little incident that touched Iona's heart—that I, a preacher, would struggle in the storm to help her light her cigarette.

The Reindeer Camp

After about eight hours of traveling, we stopped at Sownuktuk (Place of Bones). Quickly the men threw up a tent and soon the primus stove was generating a good heat. We warmed up some food, made a piping hot kettle of tea and thought we were dining at the Ritz. But this was short-lived. It was getting dark; the moon was coming up and it was time to travel.

To me the barrens are particularly beautiful in winter when they seem to be enshrouded in drifts of chaste whiteness, the hard crusts glistening in the moonlight. I love the newly fallen snow that wipes away all traces of old trails leaving a flawless, untouched landscape. There is something about the perfection, the vastness of this white wilderness stretching as far as the eye can see, unspoiled by any of the strife or problems of this world, that to me is akin to heaven.

But that night on the barrens, in spite of all the beauty surrounding us, the going was just plain hard. After many more weary hours we finally reached the reindeer herd camp a little before two in the morning—a group of four or five little tents huddled in a land of nowhere. The herders were sleeping but quickly they roused up to welcome us. These very friendly Eskimo Christians immediately received us into their tents, helping us take off our outer parkas which now had snow driven deeply into them.

How good the warmth of that little cut-down ten-gallon barrel stove felt in the tent! Our hostess Mary had cooked fresh bannock. How good it tasted as we tore off chunks to eat along with Mary's reindeer soup and hot tea.

After the long travel, we were soon drowsy and Avik, our host, suggested we turn in. Gratefully, we rolled out our sleeping bags on the reindeer skins, took off our boots and slacks and crawled in. In no time, Iona and I were both fast asleep.

Morning came all too soon. When I finally poked my head out of my bag, it was nine o'clock and Avik was already up and had the driftwood fire going. In no time the tent was warmed up and Mary was making tea. Reluctantly, I wriggled out of my sleeping bag and right away I could feel the effects of the long, hard trip. My joints and muscles were sore.

Iona spent the next day checking the babies and dealing with general health problems. As I visited in the tents, it was encouraging to see how the faith of these people was being strengthened. God responded to their simple trust, answering prayer in miraculous ways. They told me a wonderful story about Eva and William Apsimik.

At freeze-up time the reindeer camp had been moved to its new fall location. As the young ice was forming on the river a sense of peace and tranquility swept over the land. But in the Apsimik household one evening grave concern was written on every face. Eva was very ill. She had begun to hemorrhage from a miscarriage. The hemorrhage would not stop. As the hours went by the little group of Eskimo herders could do nothing. With travel impossible at freeze-up time, the camp was totally inaccessible.

But when all earthly contact ceases, the vital line of communication is still open heavenward. That evening the little band of believers crowded into Apsimik's tent and huddled around the wooden bunk where Eva was lying on the reindeer skins. The women felt her feet, then quickly drew back their hands in alarm. Her feet were cold. Her hands were cold. Eva's lips were turning blue. Only God could intervene and permit her to live.

The Christians gathered around, and quoted their favorite Scripture, "If ye shall ask any thing in my name, I will do it" (John 14:14). They began to earnestly pray. With a faith that refused to be defeated, this little band of true believers besought God to touch Eva with His wonderful healing virtue. Then they began to thank Him for what He was going to do.

The heart of God was moved by this prayer of importunity and the bleeding stopped. Eva opened her eyes. Soon her hands began to get warm, her feet warmed, and the blueness around her lips began to leave. God had touched her. She would live. How they rejoiced at the miracle-working power of their great God! Next day

The Reindeer Camp

Eva was up and around again.

Even as these herders related this story to me, it seemed to renew their faith in almighty God. We were in for a great service that evening.

I could hear a guitar in Punaktuk's tent, so obviously this was to be the meeting place. I prepared to go and then invited Iona to join us, trying to make her feel welcome without pressuring her.

"Of course I'll come, Kayy," she told me. Later on, she confided that that was one of the reasons she had wanted to come with me on the trip. Apparently the whites in Tuk were very curious about our mission and when Iona got back, the first thing they asked her was not, "Did you get cold?" but, "Did you get to a service? What was it like?"

After another day of visitation and a second service, the time came to start the long journey back to Tuk. It was very cold that morning as we prepared to leave, 58 below. The dogs moved slowly in the bitter cold, with the wind biting relentlessly.

I soon realized my feet were getting very cold. Somehow they must have become damp before we left camp, perhaps from going in and out from the tent to the toboggan. Whatever the reason, within the first hour, my feet were very, very cold. I jumped off the toboggan and ran several times, but nothing seemed to stop the increasing chill.

It is very serious to have damp feet in such low temperatures. I knew the first thing I had to do was change my socks, but I dreaded it—to expose my hands, take off the boots, the fur-lined duffles, down to my socks and finally bare skin in that stinging cold! But I knew I must. We couldn't stop for fear of losing our guide ahead, so while bouncing along on the toboggan, I gingerly pulled off my warm mitts and started the procedure. Very quickly my hands would stiffen up in the intense cold so I'd have to keep putting them back into my mitts for a brief warm-up, then take them out and try again.

Finally the task was completed and I squatted on my feet,

expecting any minute to feel new warmth. But my feet had gotten too close to freezing and they refused to respond to the dry-sock treatment. They just got colder and colder, and started to feel numb. Somehow it seemed too hard a battle to get those feet warm again. I sat on the toboggan and felt a drowsiness coming over me.

Iona was alarmed. "Kayy, I know it's tough, but I think you had better run." Even though my feet now felt like wooden stumps, I knew she was right. I must run. It was my only hope out there on the trail to keep from getting badly frostbitten.

Somehow I roused myself from this dreadful lethargy and pushed myself off the toboggan and ran and ran on those clumsy feet. When I could run no longer, I'd flop on the toboggan, take a breather, and then run some more. My numbed feet slowed my pace till I wasn't able to keep up to the team, nor was I able to jump on the toboggan any longer. I'd just sort of topple over onto it as Iona stopped the team, then we'd start up again. After half an hour of this painful, desperate procedure, I began to feel sensations in my feet. We had won the battle!

About six o'clock the men came to a little cabin on this different route that we were taking home, and quickly had a fire blazing. It was just beautiful, so warm and relaxing after the bitter chill of the day. Actually there was nothing in the cabin except a couple of rough bunks, but it was a roof over our heads, a shelter from the wind and cold, and it felt heavenly.

The men tended to the dogs, taking them out of their harness, staking them, tossing them each one frozen fish and a bit of beef tallow. The dogs howled and yelped, but eventually settled down, curled up into little balls in the snow to await another long day's haul tomorrow.

Komiak, a former reindeer herder with a tremendous sense of humor, was along on this trip, and his little jokes and witty remarks sparked our evening. But soon all of us had one thought in mind—to roll out the sleeping bags and hit the sack. Komiak took a piece of frozen meat and put it in the oven. "This will cook slowly until the fire goes out and then in the morning we'll have roast meat before we leave."

Before turning out the gas lamp, I took my Bible and quietly read a chapter and prayed. Two eyes were intently watching me, and somehow I knew that when that nurse returned to Tuk she also would start to read the Bible.

Next morning we awakened to the sounds of Komiak's blazing and crackling fire, the best possible sounds to awaken a northerner! And better yet, the air was filled with the aroma of freshly-cooked meat. Komiak had been right. The large hunk of wood had held for several hours and that little reindeer roast provided a fine breakfast feast, along with bannock and tea.

Reluctantly we began to pack our things, loath to set out in the bitter cold for the long trip home. When we started to load the sled, the dogs began barking. They knew it was time to work, but for the dogs there was no breakfast. They wouldn't be fed until evening after the day's work. These dogs would pull with all their strength for the driver on long hard trips only to be rewarded at day's end with a fish or two, a bit of blubber or a cooked "dog pot" of oatmeal and scraps. The lot of the husky sled dog always secretly bothered me.

This morning we moved quickly, working silently, all of us dreading the moment we had to leave the warmth and shelter of this deserted cabin. Had we known what the day would hold for us, perhaps we would never have started.

It was even colder, 60 below. The dogs started out at the usual fast pace, but soon their steps were slower. It was too cold even for them. Komiak and his partner left us, heading off in another direction. We shook hands. "*Ilanilu* . . . see you sometime," and soon they were black dots in the distance, leaving Nels, Iona and me to push on to Tuk.

As the day wore on, the winds became sharper, the weather seemed to warm up a few degrees and a misty ice fog settled over us. There was little daylight at that time of year—perhaps two hours—with darkness setting in shortly after noon.

We were crossing a large lake, searching for an old igloo Nels knew was there somewhere, but with the ice fog, we couldn't find it. We drove round and round, crisscrossing the lake several times, until finally in the early evening Nels stumbled onto the igloo. After traveling all day at 55 to 60 below, with a wind-chill factor that must have dropped it to 95 or 100 below, we were grateful to see this shelter. He discovered the igloo was iced up inside and consequently very, very cold.

"There's no way we can see where we're going in this dark and fog. We'll just have to wait here until the moon comes up," Nels decided.

Scrambling into the igloo, we tried to light our primus stove, but discovered that we had run out of gas. We couldn't make anything hot to drink or eat, and we had no heat. The only thing to do was to roll out the sleeping bags, crawl into them as we were, parka and all, and try to stay warm. For Nels, the skilled reindeer herder, sleeping in a cold tent or iced igloo was no problem. He simply turned over in his sleeping bag and was soon snoring.

But there was no way Iona or I could sleep, and so we just lay huddled in our sleeping bags and waited. Finally, unable to endure it another minute, I got up and poked my head out of the igloo. "The moon is up. Let's go!" I called. With this, Nels was out of his bag and harnessing the dogs.

This time we planned to keep going until we reached our home in the village of Tuk. And this was when we became completely lost and only by the help of God did we come out alive.

Later that evening, after we had again found our guide and were within sight of Tuk, I had very mixed feelings. I had not witnessed directly to Iona about her need of Christ. This strange feeling I had, to just live the Christian life before Iona and say little—had it been of God or was it my foolishness? Even cowardice? Was I ashamed to witness to another white woman? Had I missed the mark? I knew that once back in the settlement, we lived worlds apart. Her life style and mine were so totally different. I had become attached to her and wanted so much to see her become a Christian. "Oh, God, have I failed?" I wondered.

CHAPTER 13

Iona

For a few days after returning to Tuk I didn't see Iona at all. About four nights later, as I was ready to turn out the gas lamp and tuck in early, something within me said, "Keep the light on. You're going to have a special visitor."

I was so tired. I stretched out on my bunk and waited. Sure enough, in about twenty minutes I heard a little knock, and there was a rather embarrassed Iona standing in the doorway with her nurse's bag.

"Are you out on an emergency call?" I asked.

"No."

"Oh, you're just making a regular call?"

"No."

"Well, come on in," I said. Iona was always a very honest person, so right away she admitted, "Kayy, I just brought my bag along to give me courage to come. Since our trip to Husky Lakes, somehow I feel that I can talk to you. Something's bothering me inside. Can I ask some questions?"

From midnight to eight in the morning, this woman poured out the deep things of her heart, her searchings, her disappointments, her longings, her desire to know if God was really there. She told me that as a teenager she had been challenged by the gospel, but she had never made a commitment of her life to Jesus Christ. Gradually her interest in Christian things had dissipated, leaving Iona empty and disappointed, convinced that salvation was not a reality.

For most of those eight hours I just listened. The hand of God was obviously on this woman. He was dealing deeply within her soul. Before Iona left to go directly to work with no sleep, she asked if she could return the following night to discuss things further.

But that night she didn't come, nor the next. I learned that an Eskimo woman was in labor and Iona had to spend those two nights with her patient. But the third night she did come back and told me that for the past three days she had been unable to sleep or eat as the things we had discussed went over and over in her mind and heart.

"I don't feel tired or hungry. I just hurt inside," she told me.

"Iona, it's time for you to find the peace and joy that only Christ can bring." Very simply we went from Scripture to Scripture, as Iona read for herself God's wonderful plan of salvation.

Pausing once in our reading, Iona turned to me and said, "Kayy, a strange thing has happened to me. Since we came home from that trip to Husky Lakes, every night I've picked up my Bible and read a few chapters, trying to understand."

The witness that God had given me in the cabin that night was true. This woman was reading her Bible! Just before she left she said to me, "There's something I must tell you. I don't go for Pentecostal churches. Even if I do find God here, will it be all right if I don't attend your services regularly?" I assured her that attending our church was of no concern to me. The most important thing was for her to find peace with God.

Thursday night was our time for a service. Would Iona come? I purposely did not go near the nursing station that day. This decision Iona must make on her own. That night the room was packed with people; it was as though they expected something special to happen.

Suddenly the door opened and in came the nurse. One of the young people gave her a corner of the bench and she sat in the service quietly brushing away the tears that rolled down her cheeks.

When the altar call was given, inviting any to make public stand for Jesus, three or four raised their hands, and Iona raised hers. We sang verse after verse of "Just as I Am." The Eskimos came forward but Iona seemed unable to move.

Finally, at the end of the last verse, she got out of her seat, the only white woman in the congregation, stepped over the Eskimos crowding every square foot of the floor, and knelt in front of our little oil-heater altar. She gave her heart to Christ.

To the Eskimo people it was a miracle. "The white nurse has been saved!" Many mukluk feet carried the news from house to house and from tent to tent: "Even the whites are getting saved!"

After tea and another sing-song, one by one the Eskimos left. Finally about midnight I pulled on my parka and fairly ran up the hill to the nursing station. Iona was a transformed person. Never had I seen anyone so bathed in peace. It was peace she had wanted, and a double portion she had received.

She had perked a fresh pot of coffee but she didn't reach for one cigarette that night. We talked about the Lord and I explained more to her from the Bible about what had happened to her. I just couldn't seem to pull myself away from this one who so radiated the quiet peace of God. After a few hours I finally went home. Iona went to bed, and that night she slept like a baby!

First thing next day Iona visited all her white friends telling them that she had become a Christian. You can be sure this caused no small stir in that little community.

One friend responded, "Well, Iona, with something that

earth-shattering, you'd better come in for coffee and a cigarette."

But Iona replied, "That's another strange thing. Since I gave my heart to Christ, I've completely lost my desire to smoke." That shackle had been instantly broken when she surrendered to God.

A very deep and meaningful friendship began to develop between Iona and me. Little did I realize how much this woman was going to influence my life, and what a great help she would be in the Lord's work in the Arctic in days to come.

One evening while visiting me, Iona announced that she had to go home early as she had something to do. Later I pressed her to find out what this mysterious task was. Iona had felt convicted about the liquor and wine in her house. She had emptied all the bottles into a bucket and then poured it into the snow, so no one could drink it. The garbage can filled up very quickly that night with empty bottles.

A few days later she came down with two full cartons of cigarettes. "Kayy, will you do something with these? I don't want to put them in my garbage for someone else to find and use."

"How will it be if I take them out on the lake?" I suggested. "They'll make a great burnt offering to the Lord."

I noticed Iona had left an envelope on the cupboard. When I opened it, there was a check for $200. "God has been so good to me; I want to do something for Him," the little note read. Thus Iona began a ministry of giving. Giving financially and giving of herself was the great delight of Iona's Christian life.

Her hang-up about attending a Pentecostal church was soon overcome. Iona never missed a service except when she was involved with her patients. Despite the raised eyebrows and hushed remarks of her friends, Iona stood solidly with the Christians and fully identified with the Christian life in every way.

Early in her spiritual experience, Iona learned to trust God and to pray. Just three months after her conversion, a little baby was admitted to the nursing station, very sick with strange symptoms. Iona watched him carefully. The spring break-up time was upon

Iona

us, meaning that for six weeks we would be cut off from the other settlements. The planes could not land or take off. Radio communication was very poor and Iona was unable to contact the doctor in Aklavik, some ninety miles away.

After studying the case carefully, Iona confided, "Don't say anything to anyone, Kayy, but I think we have a case of typhoid fever!" In a small community like Tuk, if this were true, it would spread through the village very quickly and take many lives. "We don't have enough vaccine to inoculate all the people. I desperately need a doctor; I need his advice and more vaccine."

Day after day, the weather was socked in. Finally Iona was able to contact the doctor by radio phone, but then again she wasn't free to express what she thought the diagnosis might be, for fear of pushing the panic button. The whole community would often listen in on these conversations on their "party-line" radios. The doctor caught on to what Iona was trying to tell him and said he would do what he could.

No authorized commercial, small aircraft owner would attempt to fly in at break-up time, but there was one man who was willing to risk the trip—Don Violette. When the doctor told him of the urgency and the potential danger to the whole village, Don quickly responded, "I'll take you."

The doctor was risking the wrath of his superiors by traveling in an unauthorized aircraft, but there is tremendous dedication among the medical staff in the Arctic. More than once I've known them to stick out their necks to do what must be done, regardless of rules laid down by people five thousand miles away from the emergency. As in many times before, Don trusted his co-pilot, the Lord, to get him through. Again he made a beautiful landing and safely delivered the much-needed doctor to the community.

The doctor confirmed Iona's diagnosis. It was typhoid fever. Quickly, the whole village was immunized. There was only one other slight case reported, and with hearts full of gratitude we thanked God that a tragedy that could have taken many lives had been averted.

A few days later, a young fifteen-year-old Eskimo girl came to the nursing station in labor. This was Mabel's first baby, so the normal procedure would have been to send her to the hospital in Aklavik, but again there was no way to get her there. Iona admitted her as a patient, and then began a long vigil. Five days and nights passed with Iona by her side. Others were alarmed and concerned, but Iona kept her cool and prayed. "There's nothing we can do but pray and wait." Finally, on the sixth day, Mabel delivered a beautiful baby boy.

As long as there was a sick person, Iona's strength seemed boundless and her dedication unending. In Tuk she was regarded as the best nurse they had ever had.

CHAPTER 14

Outreach to Alaska

Throughout the winter and spring months, the house meetings had been very well attended. By June we had quite a good nucleus of believers and they felt it was high time to build a church in Tuk. The Christian men were willing to do the work if we could get drift logs out of the Mackenzie River.

There was only one man in town with a boat big enough for the job, Eddie Gruben. Eddie took it on and soon many long straight logs were piled on the bank in front of the church site. We could begin to build, but the boating season was now upon us, and for many of the men, this provided opportunity for seasonal work, loading and unloading freight boats. Our building project would just have to wait until later in the fall.

Not long after the last boat of the season steamed out of Tuk harbor, work began on the log church. Everyone helped, although most of us knew little about construction. When it came to laying tile on the floor, I think we had more glue on top of the tiles than under them. What a job to remove all that black guck!

Finally the new log church was ready. Its interior was just about as simple as you can imagine. The benches were constructed from leftover two-by-fours and strips of plywood. There was a forty-five gallon oil barrel cut down for a stove which was always hungry, constantly demanding more and more driftwood.

For a pulpit I had an upturned trunk, covered splendidly with an Indian blanket—quite an improvement over the oil space heater. Two gas lamps hung overhead. But the Holy Ghost wasn't fussy. Night after night as the people would come for services, God would bless, speak to hearts and meet many needs.

For me, it was always great to see the fall season come again because as soon as winter settled in, the Eskimo people would settle into a normal pattern of living.

That fall a new opportunity of ministry came my way when the public school opened the door for me to teach a weekly religious education class to the fifty Protestant children. Little by little, I was being accepted as a spiritual leader, and God was giving me more opportunities to serve Him.

We resumed girls' and boys' clubs, and how they enjoyed themselves! Those children were always an inspiration. No audience ever gave more rapt attention to the dramatized Bible stories than they did. No matter how bad a day I'd had, there was something about those kids and their enthusiasm that always rejuvenated me. Regardless of the handcraft or project, they were right with it. How the kids loved to make doughnuts—roll them out, cut and fry them and then serve them at one of the church gatherings.

During the fall and winter months, almost every evening about eleven o'clock a group of Eskimo young men in their late teens and early twenties would walk in, Bibles tucked in their parka pockets. We'd sit around on the floor and by gas lamp study God's Word and pray together. It was thrilling to see this group grow in God.

I could only vaguely recall the time when I found it so hard to fill up my days. Now there were four services each week, house-to-house visitation, religious education in the schools, boys' clubs, girls' clubs, women's prayer meetings, youth meetings, and individual counseling. My home was always open. People in need were always welcome and they knew it.

One day, an Eskimo Roman Catholic lady came to me. With her little girl she sat on the couch drinking cup after cup of tea. We'd talk a little, then there'd be periods of silence and waiting, more tea, more small conversation, more silence, more waiting.

Finally she blurted out, "Kayy, I know the other churches are good for clothes and to give things for the body. Your church is good for worried minds." I then queried her, "What is the problem?"

This woman, in her late forties, finally confided to me that she was going to have a baby. It was not her husband's child, and because she was older, she was ashamed. She couldn't tell the priest or the nurse. Would I tell them?

One morning as I sat in my little house preparing for services, a young Eskimo dashed in excitedly. "Kayy, there's a telephone call for you from Alaska!" Eagerly I set out across the ice to the DEW line station, a twenty minute walk. Who could it be?

The caller asked, "How about coming over to Point Barrow for some meetings?" It was Al Capener, pastor of the large Pentecostal church in Barrow. I was quite astonished, yet the invitation was heartwarming and challenging. We set the date for January, and I began to look forward to the occasion.

I traveled to Barrow via Fairbanks, and as we touched down on the packed snow landing strip I could see several Eskimo men waiting. To my surprise, as I stepped off the plane they rushed forward to greet me. "Welcome to Alaska!" This was my first introduction to the American Eskimo—outgoing, very friendly and exuberant, and quite a contrast to the hesitant shyness of the Canadian Eskimo.

In true northern style we had a service a couple of hours after arrival, and what a service it was! Many had been saved in the village of Barrow in recent years, and they had been praying fervently for this evangelistic thrust. Their faith was high. They believed God, and He responded. Night after night as the spiritual tide seemed to rise, conviction seemed to deepen. Each night souls were saved.

On about the fifth night, a group of teenagers wept their way through to God. A deep spiritual hunger was born in them, and throughout the series of meetings those teenagers were always there. If it wasn't service time, they'd come by for a Bible study or prayer meeting.

One night this group gathered around the altar after everyone else had gone home, and prayed till midnight. Still they prayed on. Some time after two o'clock several of them left the church and went out witnessing to the "night gang," a group of men and women who slept days and caroused all night.

Several men of this tough, rough gang came under deep conviction. They left their parties and poker games and headed for the church.

At 3:30 there was a knock on my door. "Kayy, there are some men here who want to get saved. Can you get up and pray with them?" I joined the pastor and showed them the plan of salvation from the Scriptures. About four o'clock they all knelt down and prayed that Jesus Christ would save their souls.

One of the men had never darkened that church door before; another was facing a court charge within a few days. "If you mean business with God," we told them, "you'll be back tonight in the service to make a public stand." We went happily to bed about six rejoicing in this unusual stir of God.

As service time rolled around that evening, we were eagerly waiting to see if these men would show up. There they were, all six of them, sitting near the front. When the invitation was given, they were the first to come forward and publicly take a stand for God.

So drastic was the change in their lives that the young man facing the court hearing was pardoned.

The tide kept rising. Some of the women involved in this night gang came to the meetings. One woman particularly attracted my attention. She'd been sitting in the back for several nights, then she began to move up a little closer. Just by looking at her I knew she had lived a hard, wild life. A love was born in my heart for her and I began to pray daily for this woman, not knowing her name.

Then one night, when she had moved about two-thirds of the way up the pews, it was obvious that God's Word was deeply stirring her heart. I saw her fighting back the tears. As the altar call was given, a battle raged within her soul. She clutched the pew ahead, wanting to go forward, yet not sure she should surrender. But God's Spirit has a wonderful way of rolling away the stones of fear and uncertainty. All at once Ruby could hold back no longer. She came running down to the altar, and in a pool of tears, humbly asked Jesus Christ to forgive her sins, change her life and make her a new person in God. As she wept there, I could only think of what Jesus said to the woman who anointed His feet: "Her sins, which are many, are forgiven; for she loved much" (Luke 7:47).

God was at work in so many lives that week. A little Eskimo girl about four years old had tugged at her father's arm in their home and said, "Daddy, let's go to church."

Charlie was a heavy drinker, but because of his little girl's constant pleading, he accompanied her to church. The next night he returned, and the next. An uneasiness and conviction of sin was growing in Charlie. He decided he wouldn't go again, but his little girl pleaded, "Daddy, take me to church." So he relented and again they went hand-in-hand to the service.

During the message, I noticed the Holy Spirit was dealing with this man. He was struggling in his heart and soul. When the altar call was given, the four-year-old turned to him, "Daddy, you need Jesus. You should go and kneel down and have a new life too." Charlie seemed to be glued to the pew, but finally he broke away and came to Christ. What a glorious night it was! A tremendous change came over Charlie.

Two years later, when the people of Barrow sent me a tape, Charlie's testimony of how he'd been delivered from drunkenness and how his life had been completely transformed rang through clearly. Nothing that we ever do for God is wasted.

The one week of scheduled meetings was extended to two weeks, and thirty more souls made decisions or commitments of their lives to Christ.

I visited a couple of other settlements, then returned to Tuk after twenty-four days in Alaska, having preached twenty-six times. This tour was a great encouragement to me personally, and lived in my heart during the hard years of pioneering that were still ahead.

CHAPTER 15

Springtime in the Arctic

Springtime is a joy in the Arctic. By May the sun is shining brightly, and the days are longer. As soon as the familiar sound of geese honking overhead is heard, there's a major exodus. The Eskimos begin to leave the villages, taking off for their spring camps at Husky Lakes. This strong desire to get out on the land is only natural after the long, cold, dark days of winter.

In springtime, the pattern of life is turned around. It's common to see little children playing outside at four and five in the morning. The adults are often out hunting, fishing, traveling, or just enjoying the long bright nights.

In the mornings, the village is dead and only a small percentage of children keep regular attendance at school during the spring months. Those who do struggle in often fall asleep at their desks. In most communities, the school system has been adapted to accommodate this spring fever, with the term ending mid-May and then beginning again in August.

This gives the families the opportunity to be together, doing what comes most naturally to them—living off their land. The Eskimos seem like different people when given the opportunity to live in their natural environment. They are so happy, so relaxed, so thoroughly interested in everything about them. Social problems are at a minimum in the camps where they are away from the drinking parties, the gambling and all that goes along with village life. Out there they are free, happy, totally enjoying their land that God has given to them.

Traveling in springtime is so very pleasant, especially at night when the snow freezes to a hard crispness. The heavy sleds, carrying supplies and gas, slide along more easily so the dogs pull better. Even the snowmobilers prefer night travel.

Though it's springtime, one must dress very warmly, wearing the usual fur boots, fur mitts, fur pants and fur parka. It's absolutely necessary to wear sunglasses during the bright spring, especially when traveling; otherwise one can quickly become the victim of very painful snow blindness. The only remedy for this is to stay in a darkened room with eyes covered until the slow process of nature's healing has taken place. This could be two days to a week depending on the severity of the injury.

I decided, "If you can't beat 'em, join 'em"—and often I would go out to their camps to fish with them and enjoy springtime, arctic style.

During one May we were surprised on a bright Sunday afternoon to see about eighteen men all clad in dress navies walking smartly across the glistening ice towards the village. I didn't know that in just a few minutes we would be treated to the pleasure of having all these men attend our Eskimo service.

They had come from the three large ships that had been frozen in the ice of the harbor all winter. Formerly United States troop carriers, these ships had been transferred to Canadian hands for summer freighting in the Arctic. Now they were being readied for this season's work, and the captain, Jack Allen, along with several members of the crew, had decided to come to church. In the north one never knows what opportunities are going to present themselves to witness for Jesus Christ.

Captain Allen was a very amiable man and one evening he graciously invited Iona and me to his ship for dinner. We had a delightful evening, once we'd slipped the two miles across the ice of the harbor and managed to climb the swinging, twenty-five-foot rope ladder up the side of the ship. (I liked it better in later years when he sent a helicopter that landed right on the deck.)

After a tour of the ship, we sat down to a delicious full course dinner in the officers' mess. Captain Allen extended this invitation to us each year. It was very pleasant for us, a time of good recreation, and we thoroughly enjoyed this touch of gracious living. Whether on the ship, in my home, or during the many times they returned for services, the captain and his crew were always perfect gentlemen, and we thanked God for their kindness to us.

At last it was time to head south for my first furlough, and I was excited at the prospect of seeing my family and friends again.

My duties in the north were to be taken over by Hugh Young, a fine Christian man from our Vancouver church, with his teenage son, Brian. During the summer they also planned to put an addition on the little house.

The Eskimo Christians were excited at the prospect of visitors from the south—at that time an unusual treat. Finally the little plane zoomed overhead, touched down on the open water and we soon were happily welcoming Hugh and Brian on their first visit to the Arctic.

After just a few days together we heard the familiar sound of the small plane overhead. It didn't take me long to pull on my jacket, grab my suitcase and be on my way for the long trip southward. I wondered how it would feel. What was this great transition going to be like?

We went as far as Aklavik where we overnighted and then waited for the larger pontoon plane, the Otter, to fly us to Norman

Wells. There we would connect with a DC-4 en route to Edmonton.

After several hours of flying, we touched down at Norman Wells. I went into the ladies' room, and there was a flush toilet—the first I had seen in three years. But somehow, modern conveniences did not seem strange. It was then I decided that much of the to-do about reentry into civilization was largely a state of mind.

As we flew along the broad Mackenzie, it was refreshing to look down and see trees again; and then over Alberta, miles and miles of neatly arranged farmland. Finally at night we came into Edmonton. After so much darkness, it was breathtaking to see the lights of a big city again.

I knew my good friends, the Browns, would be waiting for me, but somehow I wished I could just arrive alone in the night. Suddenly I felt very unsure of myself, almost embarrassed.

The Browns took me into their home and treated me royally. And here is when I discovered that I'd been too quick in deciding there was no problem with reentry into western society.

Mrs. Brown had cooked a lovely turkey, but very graciously she asked if there was anything I would especially like. In my youthful zeal I thought, here is a chance to show them that Eskimo food is quite delightful.

"I'll just have some muktuk," I announced, bringing a jar of the smelly stuff from a brown paper bag. And I proceeded to gorge myself on this arctic delicacy, much to my hostess' dismay. Too late I realized how very foolish my actions had been. (There were to be more embarrassments and difficulties this first furlough, but later I found I could slip back and forth without serious culture shock.)

Pastors Reg Layzell and Maureen Gaglardi met me when I arrived in Vancouver. It was good to be back again in the midst of the church family who had prayed so faithfully for me, and had sacrificed so willingly to enable us to reach the Eskimos for Christ.

So often the memory of their love had warmed and encouraged me. I felt free to share with them those deep desires God had placed in my heart to reach out even further with the gospel. In my home church and wherever I went, the response was great, with a deep concern shown in the hearts of God's people for this pioneer field beyond the Arctic Circle.

My aging mother was overjoyed to see me home safe and sound, and I was equally happy to see her, if only for seven short weeks.

Everyone was so gracious and friendly and warm-hearted towards me; yet soon I felt a restlessness coming over my spirit, a desire to return to what had become my true home—the Arctic. I knew now there was no glamour in the north, but the desire to return and serve those people was a living passion with me.

Finally the morning of departure came, and this time it was even harder to leave my dear mother. With tears I kissed her good-bye, then hurried to the pastor's car. For several minutes I just sat quietly looking out the window, trying to get hold of my emotions. At the airport, even though it was early morning, several church people had come to see their missionary off to the field again.

And then May Robbins, a dear, old, white-haired lady who lived on a mere pittance and served the Lord by cleaning the church, shook my hand and slipped me a bill. I glanced down. Five dollars! I knew it was probably all that she had.

Her face was beaming as she said from her heart, "Kayy, I want you to have it." Months later, this act of sacrificial love lived in my heart, but that morning in the Vancouver airport, I felt myself becoming unglued. Fortunately, they were calling my flight number. It was time to go aboard. The group gathered around me to pray and when we opened our eyes, the loading ramp had been lifted. As I dashed out, they lowered it again. I waved a final good-bye, and then I was off, bound for the northland again.

The Eskimo people enthusiastically welcomed me home again, as perhaps only they can. In their warm way they made me feel like the most important person in the whole village.

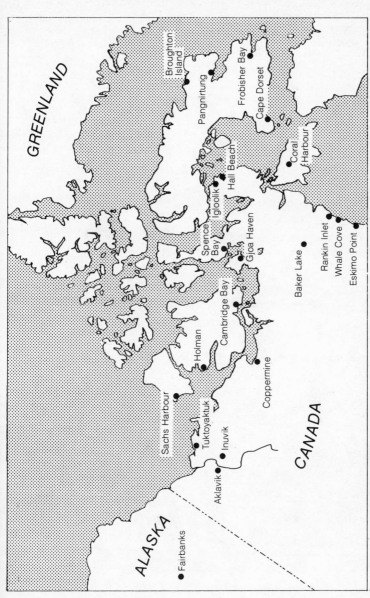

Arctic settlements we've reached with the gospel. Many more villages await the Good News.

Paul, the Eskimo evangelist.

My dog team—faithful companions on many a long journey.

The bombardier at Coral Harbour.

A successful polar bear hunt.

Children of the Arctic—God's "treasures in the snow."

The church at Cambridge Bay.

The arctic reindeer.

Our long-awaited, five-seater Cessna 185.

Cambridge Bay–Reaching Out

CHAPTER 16

The Settlement

With the work in Tuk well established, I felt it was God's time for me to forge farther across the arctic coast to once again pioneer with the gospel of power through Jesus Christ.

The target was Cambridge Bay, a poor settlement on the bleak shores of Victoria Island, some 20 miles north of the Arctic Circle and 800 miles east of Tuk.

My compelling desire and prayer was that not only would they find Jesus Christ as Savior and Lord, but also that they might enter into the fullness of Holy Ghost joy and power so desperately needed in this harsh land.

Mike and Rose Chamaschuk of Edmonton had presented themselves as missionary candidates to the Arctic, and now they were ready to take over the work at Tuk, freeing me to push eastward.

As I prepared to go among people I had never seen before, there was a certain amount of anticipation, a thrill about this forthcoming adventure. I was secretly hoping that Sophie would accompany me to Cambridge Bay. But it seemed that while I was away in Alaska, she had fallen in love with a young Eskimo from Aklavik.

As she told me about him, I could see Sophie very much wanted to be married, to have a home of her own and take her place as a wife and mother. Of course I agreed with this, but it meant that once again, I would have to face things alone.

I continued to pack, but my heart was heavy and my pace slowed. Iona had left Tuk for a government nursing position at Watson Lake in the Yukon. It seemed strange not having her around, but this is the way of the north. The pangs of loneliness began to creep in once more, but superseding all else was this great desire to push east.

After the Chamaschuks arrived in Tuk, we had a few weeks to acquaint them with the mission and the people. Then the evening of my farewell service came, much too quickly. I hadn't realized it would be so difficult to leave the people of Tuk. I had grown very attached to them and many had expressed their appreciation for my years of ministry there.

I'd made arrangements to travel to Cambridge Bay by DEW line plane, but as so often in the north, the weather delayed us. Finally, on the fifth day of waiting, the DEW line truck drove up to my door. The aircraft was coming soon. My belongings were loaded in the back of the truck: a suitcase, sleeping bag, small tent, primus stove and a few other camping items, and that was just about it.

We were scheduled to arrive in Cambridge Bay after dark. How would I manage, I wondered. I didn't know a soul in town, and it's difficult to set up a tent at night. I just prayed, "Lord, make a way."

When we touched down, the DEW line bus driver inquired, "Where are you planning to stay?" Suddenly I remembered Rosie, the daughter of a reindeer herder. She was married now and living in Cambridge Bay. Following a visit with her family at Reindeer Station, Rosie had had to wait in Tuk for a plane, and she and her four children had spent a few days with me.

"Could you drop me off at Rosie Tologonak's house?" I asked.

We took off into the night, driving the three miles from the airport and then through the village, a hodgepodge of little shacks straggling out over quite an area. Finally we arrived at a little hut on the side of a hill. I asked the driver if he'd wait just a moment while I made sure I could camp with Rosie for the night.

Understandably, she was very surprised to see me on her doorstep at midnight. She had no idea I was coming, but with typical Eskimo grace, she quickly said, "Sure, you're welcome. Just bring your things."

As I stood at Rosie's door, I noticed that the familiar grey blanket was on the floor with cards, money, cigarettes, all kinds of loot—a big poker game was obviously in progress. But during the time it took me to run back to the truck and return to the house, an amazing transformation took place. They'd scooped all the cards under the chairs, thrown the blanket in the corner, and now everyone was sitting up on benches smiling, just as if they'd been visiting all evening. I pretended not to notice anything unusual and went around shaking hands Eskimo style. After a few minutes, they started to leave one by one.

Finally only Rosie, her children, and I were left in the house. "Rosie, what in the world did you say to them that suddenly broke up that big poker game?" I asked.

Rosie shrugged. "I just told them that Kayy Gordon (*Minihituk*—'preacher') had arrived from Tuk. They just stopped playing themselves."

Rosie laughed. "Isn't it nice to have a quiet house at last? Now we can have a nice visit." Some of the men came back a few hours later to pick up their loot, but most of it was left until morning.

As Rosie and I visited and drank tea together, a deep sense of gratitude welled up in my heart for this home that had been opened so graciously to me. We talked till the wee hours of the morning and when I finally lay snugly in my sleeping bag rolled out on a caribou skin on Rosie's kitchen floor, my heart was singing, "Bless the Lord, oh my soul, and all that is within me, bless His holy name."

Again, He had demonstrated to me that He always goes before His people. In the wilderness and strange land where there is no way, He always makes a way. The floorboards were hard beneath me, but it was shelter from the dark night and cold. Rosie's warm welcome made me feel so comfortable.

The next morning I was anxious to explore the village where I planned to spend quite a few years. Squatting on the south shore of Victoria Island with the wind whipping in off the Arctic Ocean, Cambridge Bay seemed so very bleak, with rock everywhere. There was no sign of the beautiful, multi-hued tundra of the Mackenzie Delta area.

In those days, Cambridge Bay seemed to be a settlement with no core or unity. After the government had built a nursing station and the social development department and day school, with the DEW line station just three miles away, the nomadic Eskimos had drifted in. Yet each camp had kept to themselves with the result that the village straggled over quite an area.

In one far part of town, some Perry River people had assembled a little group of shacks built mostly from crating boxes salvaged from garbage at the DEW line site. The Bathurst Inlet people had set up their "camp," again poorly constructed houses built from scraps scrounged from the DEW line dump.

And so it was throughout the settlement, several different groups of Eskimos clustering together as they had in their camps. Thus no strong Eskimo leadership had emerged. When I arrived, the total population was only three hundred Eskimos and about fifty whites.

I spent the first few days in Cambridge walking around the settlement, shaking hands with as many people as I could. I had ordered lumber to build a small house, but while I waited for the supply ship, I pitched my little tent behind Rosie's house. Sitting down on the caribou skin and picking up my little tenor guitar, I began singing gospel songs.

After a few minutes I could hear feet walking on the rough stones, approaching the tent. I was about to have some visitors. A group of children ranging in age from about ten to thirteen years, appeared at the door and very shyly stepped in. They were curious about the songs they had heard from outside the tent. This music was my first contact with the people.

The first school had been started a year before I arrived, so these children were able to speak English and they quickly learned the gospel songs. Day after day they came by my tent and no matter what I was doing, I would always lay it aside, pick up the guitar and play and sing.

The children of Cambridge Bay were classically beautiful with their fat cheeks, pug noses and golden brown skin. Their happy little faces were framed with the fur ruff of their parkas. Although more shy than the children at Tuk, I found them warm and responsive, so easy to befriend. Their black eyes would sparkle with delight at any special attention.

The gospel songs spread like wildfire through the village. A few weeks later when I was in the Hudson's Bay store I heard someone humming, "I'm so glad Jesus lifted me." My curiosity got the better of me so I strolled over that way and there was the Hudson's Bay manager, Bill Heslop, that seasoned trader of the north, humming the little chorus he had heard so often in the store. Everywhere I went in the village, these little choruses had preceded me.

One thing was unique about this particular summer. This was the "Year of the Lemming" (a little, heavily-furred, mouse-like creature that has a habit of getting in everywhere it shouldn't). Their population increases in roughly four-year cycles, and this was a peak summer. The tundra was swarming with them.

When I pitched my tent, I became very aware of the lemming problem. I managed to obtain a couple of pieces of old plywood to lay as a floor on top of the rocks, but the unevenness created a teeter-totter effect. As I would step on one edge of the plywood, a lemming would dart out the other side. When I reached into the orange crate cupboard that was sitting precariously on one side of the tent, out would jump a lemming. They were just everywhere—scooting across the table, in the frying pan, under the floor, over the bed, into my boots. I felt as if I was in Egypt during one of the plagues!

If there's one thing that I cannot abide, it's a rodent, in any shape or variety. What a challenge this superabundance of lemmings was to me personally. Before going to bed I would very gingerly unroll my sleeping bag, and then very slowly and carefully put my hand inside to check for lemmings.

Those first weeks at Cambridge Bay I realized would be critical ones, for many Eskimo eyes were watching me. Most single white women in the north get caught up in a round of social life, often getting deeply involved with the opposite sex. Almost immediately a problem developed that I had to conquer if I wanted the Eskimos to know that I did not intend to follow this pattern of behavior. I had only had my tent up for a day or two when a truck drove up with four men from the DEW line station. "Hi, Kayy, just thought we'd drop by to say hello. Is there anything we can help you with?" Of course I invited them in and made coffee. After an hour or two they left. The next night there was another local vehicle in front of the tent.

This could not go on, because it would almost certainly be misread by the native people. But what was I to do? I couldn't be rude to people who were simply trying to be kind to me.

Finally I hit on a solution. Each evening I would go out visiting or walking, and just be out in case the boys might come calling. In this way I would not be a stumbling block to the native people whom I had come to help.

Walking has never been a delight to me, but night after night I would take off for a long hike. Sometimes I'd climb the hill and if the coast was clear, I'd return to my tent. After a while I bumped into one of the fellows in the store.

"Funny thing, Kayy, you're never home in the evenings anymore," he said. "You're not trying to avoid us, are you?" I just smiled and said nothing. I felt badly about this apparent snubbing because over the years, the DEW line personnel always rallied to help me by arranging transportation, repairing equipment, helping with construction. They were always so generous and helpful.

The summer passed quickly, between dodging the lemmings, singing with the children whenever they popped into my tent, and visiting around the community.

One day, in late August, the school principal approached me: "Kayy, would you be interested in helping us with the school pickup?" Each fall, children from outlying villages were brought to Cambridge Bay en route to the large hostel schools in Inuvik. During the waiting period, while all the children were being collected, the youngsters slept on mattresses. These were rolled out in the classrooms which also served as the dining area.

It was a dreadfully congested situation, and it must have been traumatic for youngsters to leave home and their loved ones to be huddled together in this temporary situation. But as is so typical of Eskimo children, they adjust very readily. Their attitude and spirit was so great, as they would say with a shrug, *"ayonakman"*-"because it cannot be helped."

There was difficulty in getting staff for this operation, to prepare the meals, serve them and so on. I was delighted with the opportunity to pitch in and help with a community problem. As well, this gave me a chance to meet children from outlying areas that I one day hoped to visit.

When the children arrived at Cambridge Bay, they were given food, a bath, hair wash, and medical check-up at the nursing station. As one new group of children tumbled in, one little fellow who by now was all slicked up, came over to me and said, "Boy, don't these guys stink!'' Little did he realize that a few hours earlier he'd been in the same condition.

Many came in with nothing but the clothes on their backs. I recall one little girl whose mother had made her a brand new pair of sealskin boots in the springtime. Sealskin tends to shrink when it gets wet, and by the time this child reached Cambridge Bay in late August, we had to cut away her boots from her feet. Obviously she had not had them off for months.

What did we feed these 125 ravenous youngsters? For breakfast it was usually three big pots full of rolled oats. The Eskimo staff whipped up huge quantities of bannock to serve with jam and tea. Eskimo children are accustomed to drinking tea and enjoy it immensely. Lunch would be soup, and tinned fruit or jello for dessert, and the familiar pilot biscuits. For supper we would have beans or macaroni with lots of sliced canned meat, some kind of a pudding or fruit, and hot chocolate.

Sometimes they were weathered in for days; one year it was for two weeks. Finally the big plane buzzed the village. The children were hurried into the DEW line bus, as well as every other vehicle in the village that rolled, and transported the three miles to the airport. Suddenly the commotion was over, the school quiet. The fall pickup had been completed for another year.

CHAPTER 17

Igloo Pinektok

One big difference in Cambridge Bay was the relentless, driving wind. My tent flapped and flapped. Any day now the freight ship should be in, the last ship of the season. If my supplies were not on it, I would indeed be in difficulty. Winter in a tent in the comparatively sheltered area of Reindeer Station was one thing, but here on this bleak, wind-swept shore? I shuddered, then raised my heart to God, ". . . Hitherto hath the Lord helped us" (1 Sam. 7:12).

Finally, far out in the distance, the Eskimos sighted a little speck moving on the water. The freight ship! Before the ship had docked, we all made our way to the shore. And as soon as possible I found the purser. Had my supplies made it?

Thank God! All the lumber and materials were on board! They would be unloaded in a day or two and then I could begin building the small shack that would serve as house and chapel.

As I worked on the building, the winds became sharper and

137

colder and blew constantly. It was only early September, yet I had to wear my muskrat parka, and my hands became red and stiff from the intense cold.

One day when I was trying to pound four-inch spikes into some uprights, I missed and hit my finger which was already stinging and burning with the bitter cold. It was almost too much. I remember thinking to myself, what kind of fool am I, trying to do a man's job under such impossibly adverse circumstances? Why don't I pack it up? The weather in Vancouver is pretty nice in September. Even the job in the dental office had to be an improvement over this madness. Just what was I trying to prove?

But just as quickly, as though it were an answer to me, the Scripture flashed into my mind: "For God is not unrighteous to forget your work and labour of love, which ye have showed toward his name" (Heb. 6: 10). That verse melted my heart. "Forgive me, Lord, but help me," I prayed desperately as I grabbed the hammer in numb hands and went at those spikes again.

Many Eskimos would come to watch, and sometimes it bothered me that big strong men could stand with hands in their pockets and say, "Igloo *pinektok*–nice house," and then walk away as I was struggling to saw a two-by-six. But whenever they came to visit, I would always lay down my tools and invite them into the tent for a cup of tea. Then I would pick up the guitar and play and sing a few choruses in Eskimo. In this way a friendly rapport was established long before I got down to formally presenting the gospel message.

They marveled that a white woman, who lived in a tent like an Eskimo, would do something very strange for even an Eskimo woman—build a house. Oftentimes I worked very long hours from early morning till midnight by the light of a gas lantern. When I was too tired to work any longer, I'd put the tools away, have a cup of tea, a quick wash and then crawl into the sleeping bag.

After much struggle, the underfloor was laid, insulated, and the final floor nailed down. Then a group of Eskimo men helped me turn it over.

Next came the frame. I knew I couldn't handle upright studding by myself, so I decided to build all four sides on the ground, and then get help to lift them in place. I didn't know it, but apparently this is the procedure that most contractors used in such a building project.

One morning I awakened to an unusual stillness. Cautiously, I looked out of the tent and was astonished to see the bay shimmering with young ice. And this was just the first week of September! An early freeze-up had come. I realized I would have to work feverishly to get the building enclosed.

About the end of September, when the whole country was blanketed in snow and the ice on the bay was thick enough to walk on, the task of framing the walls was finally completed. That evening some men helped me stand up the walls; we nailed the four sides together, and now it looked more like a house, even if it was still roofless.

Roof work frightened me. I couldn't cope with heights, so I decided to spend my last hundred dollars to hire two men for the job. I was able to find an oil space heater, so just as soon as the roof was on, a few windows were in and the door was hung as best we could, I left the cold, windy tent and moved into my new house. Not only would I be warm, but there would be another great advantage—no lemmings running across my face as I slept!

Most of the house would serve as a fourteen-by-sixteen-foot chapel. Six feet across one end would be my own living quarters, consisting of a six-by-five-foot bedroom, a six-by-eight-foot kitchen-dining-living area, and a corner for the "honey bucket." After several weeks of continual plugging away at it, the interior was finally finished, the walls were painted and a piece of linoleum from the Hudson's Bay was laid on the chapel floor.

At last we were ready for our opening service. I wondered how many people would come. I had not had the time to invite anyone. To my delighted surprise, Rosie Tologonak had done a great job of informing everyone that our grand opening would be in the evening at seven.

The chapel was soon packed with Eskimos. They were full of curiosity. What did this strange white woman have to say? What was this gospel of Jesus Christ? They had been well-churched. Anglican and Catholic churches had been there for years. But most of the Inuit had never seemed to grasp the simple gospel truths that could lead them to a personal knowledge and enjoyment of salvation, a salvation that changes lives and transforms sinners into good parents and good citizens.

Their concept of a Christian was a do-gooder who goes to church on Sunday. When the scheduled plane came in once a month with its load of liquor, it was a common sight the next day and the next night to see almost every Eskimo family drunken, passed out at their parties, with their children bewildered and crying, not knowing what had happened to mom and dad. Yet these same people would be in their churches Sunday after Sunday.

That first night in our little chapel we sang a few gospel songs and choruses in both English and Inuktuk and then I gave a simple gospel message. Pointing to the black cover of my Bible, I emphasized how awful sin is and how it destroys a person's relationship with God. I told them how much God loved us, how He sent Jesus to die on the cross, to shed His blood so that we might have forgiveness. I offered them the hope that our hearts can be as white as the white pages in my Bible. Many were very interested; some were stunned. "We never heard it like that!" they exclaimed.

After the short service, I invited them to stay for tea and doughnuts. Then I picked up the guitar and we sang some more gospel choruses. How they reveled in these! Here was I, very unmusical by nature, yet in desperation I had learned to strum a four-string tenor guitar, and with that we started the gospel work in Cambridge Bay.

When they left that night, I lay on my bunk with the gas lamp burning brightly overhead, the oil stove rumbling comfortingly, the wind and snow blowing outside. But how warm, cozy and contented I was. My heart was so full and overjoyed at the opportunity God had given me. Tired, yes. A little lonely, yes. But within there was a deep satisfaction of having begun something that I knew God was going to bless.

A few nights later I had an unexpected visit from three clerks at the Hudson's Bay. One of the three, Peter, a young Englishman, who boarded in the manager's home, asked me several thoughtful questions concerning our message and faith. Obviously, he was searching for the truth.

Peter returned alone a couple of nights later and from God's Word I showed him that there is no back door into heaven. I told him that he would have to come to God unashamedly and make a public confession. Only then can the reality of salvation truly grip a person's heart and life.

The next Sunday night, with the chapel already packed beyond capacity, a vehicle drove up with some of the DEW line officials—the superintendent, the dentist, some supervisors, and their friend, Babs Heslop, wife of the Hudson's Bay manager. Peter also came. Somehow we managed to squeeze everyone into the chapel.

That night as I again preached the simple gospel, the Holy Spirit was faithful to convict the people of their need of God. Peter's heart was pricked. He had told me he would like to listen a few times before he made a decision, but in this very first service God got ahold of him. I invited anyone who wanted to make a public stand for Christ to come and kneel in an area that had been cleared for prayer. In front of his boss's wife, in front of the DEW line officials, in front of a whole houseful of Eskimos, Peter came forward and knelt down, committing his life to Christ.

The Eskimos were stirred. "This must be good. Even the white man gets saved. He beats us!" they said among themselves.

Peter had received a real experience from the Lord that changed his life. Now he had fulfillment and meaning in his life. During the next months he took his stand undauntedly as a Christian young person in the community, helping others find Jesus Christ.

The people in Cambridge Bay were quite different in many ways from the people in Tuk. Their standard of living was not as high. By and large their homes were little shacks thrown together from the garbage dump. Seal blubber was used for fuel in many makeshift stoves—crude, cutdown ten-barrel drums. The smell of seal blubber penetrated their clothes and boots. Very often after a service it was necessary to wash all the benches and the floor because the smell of seal would sometimes linger in the building for hours.

But these things were not important. My great desire was to reach the people and constantly I invited them to visit me in my home. Soon they felt quite free to come and go. One day I kept track. Starting at about eleven in the morning and continuing through the day until two o'clock the next morning, over thirty people visited, with never less than six visitors at any time. A continuous stream of people for fifteen hours! But this was the Eskimo way of life.

The days rolled into weeks and soon it was just about Christmas time. That first Christmas in Cambridge Bay fell on a Sunday, and as usual the other churches had gone all out. That Christmas was not one that I would mark as a red letter day in my life. There were only two people in our service on Christmas day. Everyone else had gone to the other churches as a matter of tradition. It was a very trying, lonely experience, but somehow I knew that when Christmas rolled around again, there would be a dramatic change.

CHAPTER 18

God Breaks Through

The bitterly cold month of January was upon us. By now I thought I knew all about arctic winters, but that January in Cambridge Bay was something else. The winds never seemed to stop blowing and it was intensely cold, much colder than Tuk. But regardless of the wind or weather, I made it a practice to go out every day, visiting and keeping in contact with the people.

Peter was growing in God by leaps and bounds. But why weren't the Eskimo people responding to Christ? I began to wonder if the problem was with me. "Perhaps I can't relate to them. Maybe I've missed the will of God. Maybe I'm kidding myself, and I'm not really called to these people after all," I began to think. For the first time since I had come into the Arctic four-and-a-half years before, serious doubts clouded my mind. I was deeply discouraged, and for the first time in my missionary life I seriously wanted to quit.

True, there had been that time in Tuk when I returned to my tent and found the nest of baby mice and impetuously wanted to head south. But this time I wanted to chuck over everything—the Arctic, the ministry—and just be an ordinary Christian holding down a job where there weren't so many problems to face. What was the use anyway? My patience, for which I was never noted, was being severely tried.

Finally, in desperation one Sunday in February, I prayed, "Lord, if you can't save a goodly number of Eskimos through my ministry by the end of June, I'm quitting." And I meant every word of it.

That night the church again was packed. The little room could hold no more. At the end of the service, I again gave an invitation for any who would like to accept Christ. That night, "the crack in the ice" came loud and clear. Nine Eskimos raised their hands for prayer, and nine made their way to the front where we managed to clear an area for them to kneel and give their hearts to Jesus Christ.

My interpreter was not a Christian, and I couldn't speak the dialect of these people. So I had no choice but to lead them to Christ through an unsaved interpreter. How in the world the interpreter managed not to get saved is still a mystery to me! At the end of the day I sank to my knees and wept before God, truly grateful for this breakthrough in the hearts of the people.

The next Sunday the place was packed even more than the Sunday before. One visitor counted eighty-two heads in our little fourteen-by-sixteen-foot chapel area. The heat in the room was not caused by the oil stove, for I had turned it off. But with so many human bodies together in one place, there was real sweat in the Arctic that night. Six more Eskimos raised their hands, but that night there was just absolutely no way for them to move out of their place.

One of these was Analok, a trapper who had gone on the DEW line where he'd become a heavy drinker and gambler. He'd recently quit his work and returned to Cambridge Bay and now he had found the Lord. Analok and the others testified to the great change that Jesus had made in their lives. They had lost the desire to drink. Already they had found a better life, a happier life. They didn't want to follow the old, sinful ways of drinking, gambling and running around. Now they only wanted to follow Jesus Christ and live for Him.

These events electrified the whole town. Conversions were talked about in the Eskimo homes and reportedly became a topic of conversation even at white parties. What was this gospel of power that was changing lives? Many came to our services out of curiosity.

About the same time I realized the location of the building was not central enough. I had tried unsuccessfully to secure a land lease, but the government official was hesitant. A proper survey was planned for the whole village but that would not be until August. We had to do something sooner than that. I decided to try the government office one more time.

The first official was out of town and his assistant seemed much more lenient. "Let's put it this way," he suggested. "If a building suddenly appeared on a lot in the center of town during the night, I don't think we would move it in the morning."

I thanked him and immediately went about bracing the building, preparing it for a move. It had been erected on skids with the thought of one day moving it and this was our cue. Within a couple of days arrangements were made for a tractor to pull the building over to its new location; in just an hour's time the job was done. The building was sitting on a ridge overlooking the bay, an ideal location.

How good God is to those who put their trust in Him! The people appreciated the fact that we were now close and they could drop in on their way to and from the Hudson's Bay store.

"She buys by her eyes," they'd tell me as we sat drinking tea. That meant she bought what caught her eyes. "He's bad for muktuk," or "he's bad for that girl" meant he was crazy about muktuk or that girl. I enjoyed these friendly visits as much as they did.

A new problem was facing me. We had about twenty converts, most of whom could speak only a little English. And I could not yet speak their dialect. We needed someone who would be a good interpreter and a good worker among the Eskimos.

As I prayed about this, one man came to my mind especially—John Maksagak, a very gentle but steady Christian, one who loved God and loved His people, and who had prayed many times from the depths of his heart for the people in the east.

But John had a good job in Inuvik, with a modern, comfortably-furnished home. John also had a large family. Would he consider moving to the east, leaving all that behind to serve the Lord?

Finally I wrote him a letter telling him of the great need. Would he pray about it? One month later, on the next plane, there was an answer from John.

"Praise the Lord, Kayy," he wrote. "Oh, yes, I'll come. Don't you remember the word of the Lord in prophecy that was spoken over me at the reindeer round-up four years ago? That God would send me to the east and that I would minister to those people?"

I had completely forgotten about that prophecy, but obviously John hadn't. He had patiently waited for the hour when God would fulfill it.

John set about putting things in order, quit his job, sold most of their belongings at half price, and prepared to pack up his wife and five children and head for Cambridge Bay with a few suitcases and a little trunk. Just before he was to leave Inuvik, his wife, Helen, became ill and was taken to Edmonton for further tests. His youngest child, Bonnie, only one year old, also became desperately ill in Inuvik, but John believed God. Nothing could stop him from answering this call to the east.

He visited the hospital and there prayed for his baby, committing her into God's hands, and trusting that she would soon rejoin the family. Such was the faith of this man.

Against the advice of his close friends and relatives, John set his face eastward. It was a very cold afternoon when the DEW line plane arrived and there was John with four of his children. No wife, no baby—but a smile on his face and a "Praise the Lord" on his lips, and a faith in his heart because he felt he was answering the call of God, and that all things were in His hands.

That evening John shared with the people his great faith in God. For John, God was real and alive! Hadn't John proved it so many times?

These young Christians in Cambridge Bay wept with joy as John told them of his many miraculous deliverances. One time John was out alone on the tundra herding the reindeer when suddenly he saw a huge brown bear charging towards him. John had no weapon in his hands, no means of defense. So strong was his faith that he did not turn and run. Rather, John fell to his knees facing the bear, closed his eyes and lifted his arms to heaven. "In Jesus' name, help me," he simply cried. The bear stopped in his tracks, abruptly turned and disappeared over the hill.

Another day John was alone at the herd tent, chopping driftwood for a fire. Somehow the axe slipped and deeply gouged his foot. The blood began to spurt out. John immediately thought of his wife and little children back home. He put his hand on his bleeding foot and prayed, "In Jesus' name, let this bleeding stop so I can make it back to my family. Oh, God, don't let me die. My wife and children need me."

The flow of blood subsided. John tied a rag around his foot and began the long walk of several miles back to the camp. At times he became very faint from the initial loss of blood, and beside the trail he again prayed for strength to go on. The bleeding did not start again, and this deep wound healed quickly. Like Kailek and Eva, John knew the Great Physician had touched him on the tundra.

When John arrived we had no home for him. I welcomed them to stay with me and this was the way we lived for many months, all of us together in the little sixteen-by-twenty-foot home that also doubled as a chapel.

In a few weeks' time, Helen joined her husband and family, flying in from the hospital in Edmonton. And after another few weeks young Bonnie was sent home from the Inuvik hospital. How they rejoiced to be all together again! They didn't have many earthly things, but they were rich in love and devotion and the desire to serve God and their own people.

For a family of seven (with another on the way) to move into my little house required a good deal of adjustment for everyone. John and Helen took over the little five-by-six-foot bedroom; and four of the children slept with me in the chapel. During the day the chapel also had to serve as dining and living room, but at night we moved the backless benches together, laid caribou skins across, rolled out the sleeping bags and there we all slept. This meant absolutely no privacy, but one learns to navigate around these circumstances.

Of the five children, four were preschoolers, so our little home churned with constant activity. Perhaps this was the hardest adjustment for me, for I was used to quietness and solitude, at least at times when we had no visitors. Now this was a literal impossibility.

As the weeks and months wore on, it became evident to me that I had to find some place where I could have quietness to study, meditate and pray. Right next to our property there was a tiny, vacant building belonging to the Hudson's Bay Company.

I asked the manager if I could buy it, but he replied, "You can just have it." And so John and I set about making this five-by-six-foot matchbox habitable. We had some insulation left over for the walls. There was no plywood or interior sheeting, but I remembered a trick from depression days on the farm—using flattened out cardboard boxes for wallboard. John built a bunk and made a little cupboard for my books and papers.

The little shack had been used as an ammunition depot, and with no windows it was rather dark and dreary. But to me it was the next thing to heaven for when I entered that little place there was peace and quiet. The primus stove heated the small area quickly, but the moment the stove went out, the room became very cold. The bunk was not long enough for me to stretch out on, but I remember my delight when I curled up in my little bunk in what was soon dubbed, "Kayy's little house." There I could thank the Lord for again helping me in my time of need.

CHAPTER 19

The Flesh Is Weak

One morning I woke up feeling hot and flushed and sick to my stomach. I decided to ignore it and maybe it would go away, but in a few short hours I found myself lying down again on my bunk. Then incessant vomiting started. This was unusual because I was just never sick.

After a couple of days I decided I'd better move back to the benches in the chapel where at least there was continuous heat during the night. Still I didn't improve. In fact I grew worse. I lay on the caribou skins on top of those benches, wondering, what can this sickness be? It's an uneasy feeling to become unaccountably ill in the Arctic. By now I knew only too well how often it is impossible to fly out, how many delays there can be—often fatal delays.

It became obvious that I could not be in church that Sunday and I would have to vacate my bed in the chapel. We arranged for John to take the service, and the Bocks, a Christian family in town, extended loving hospitality to me. Their little boy gave up his bedroom, and I had to admit that lying in a real bed with a real mattress, between nice clean sheets, felt mighty good. I just lay there, totally enjoying such luxury.

During the first seven days of illness I lost eleven pounds. Helen called the nurse, but I decided it was just the flu so I phoned the nurse back and told her she really didn't need to come. (Actually I was embarrassed to have her see our living conditions.)

But now at Bocks' home I had to admit that I was a sick girl. The nurse came, whisked me off to the nursing station and put me into bed, much to my dismay. The DEW line doctor was to come and examine me. Somehow he didn't make it, so I had to remain overnight at the nursing station.

After the examination, the DEW line doctor told me the news: I had a bad case of infectious hepatitis. It wouldn't be fatal, but because I had a severe case it would take me a long time to recover. In the meantime they insisted that I stay another week in the nursing station for the balance of the contagious period. I tried to smile, but inside my heart sank. "Oh, God, why did this have to happen, and why now?" I questioned.

Unknown to the doctor or the nursing staff, I was facing another very serious problem. It was very difficult for our mission office in Vancouver to grasp any concept of the high cost of living in the Arctic and this was leading to some difficult misunderstandings. That winter we had run out of fuel oil simply because I had had no idea how much colder Cambridge Bay was than Tuk. Consequently, I hadn't ordered in a large enough supply by barge.

When our supply was exhausted, I had no alternative but to purchase fuel oil from the Bay, at a cost of $1.65 per gallon. This shoved our monthly fuel bill to over $300 just to heat our 320 square feet. When Pastor Layzell saw this figure, he could only conclude that I must be giving away fuel oil to the less fortunate native people. Other similar incidents had triggered a rather sensitive situation between the office and me.

Just prior to becoming ill, a letter had arrived from my pastor informing me that our missionary budget simply could not stand the stretch of these extra dollars. It was already overtaxed. I would either have to ''cut these extravagances'' or else assume responsibility for my own finances. I had decided to choose the latter of the two suggestions. I would go south and raise funds not only for my own support, but also for John and his family until such time as he was able to get local employment.

My reply to Vancouver stating this decision had just been mailed. Now I was stricken with hepatitis. As I lay in the nursing station, each day seemingly growing worse, I began to wonder what this was all about. Was God chastening me for my impatient, willful attitude, impetuous reaction, and stubborn independence? How were things going to work out now?

Because I felt so ill, I somehow just committed it all to God and said, ''Lord, have mercy on me. Forgive me my foolishness and somehow get me out of this mess.''

The nursing staff in Cambridge Bay treated me very well. But I was still uncomfortable, feeling that the nursing station was basically for the Eskimos and I was an added burden. After ten days I was discharged and the Wilsons, a kindly white couple, took me into their home for a few more days of recuperation.

Back home again, we began working on the chapel extension that had been started before my illness. We desperately needed more space. Now as I tried to drive those spikes into the ceiling joists, I could hardly get one spike in without tremendous weakness and excruciating pain. I'd lie down for an hour and then work for two. Finally, after a few days, the old liver pain and nausea returned. With this, the nurses told me it was either go south to recuperate properly, or, if I insisted on persevering, I could expect a total relapse.

To make things more difficult, the strain between the Vancouver office and myself had not lessened. It is just amazing what towering mountains of misunderstanding can develop with a lack of communication. But hearing of my illness, the pastor urged me to come home.

I went south on the DEW line plane with a heavy heart, and a sick body. However, I chose to go east to my relatives whom I had not seen for several years, hoping to recuperate a little before going on to Vancouver. Having lost fifteen pounds, I looked pretty peaked.

My sister took me to a doctor and after examining me he said, "Kayy, you're dangerously near a complete relapse. I'd like to put you in the hospital. There's no way you can do any preaching."

Still I refused to give in. I was planning some strenuous travel to various churches to raise support for John and me in case my differences with the mission proved to be irreconcilable.

Then I received word again from Vancouver. "You really must come so that we can clarify these matters." Finally I accepted this as God's will and was soon on my way.

During long talks in his study, Pastor Layzell suggested a principle of problem solving that would become a very important factor in my life.

"Kayy, there is no way we can ever iron out between us who is right and who is wrong on all these individual matters," he said. "Let's just forget the past and start afresh. And we do want to continue your support."

So we buried the past, and started fresh with a new financial arrangement. Instead of an expense account, I was given a monthly stipend to stretch as best I could, but with no accounting required.

I have always been very grateful for the wisdom the pastor showed. Not only did it resolve our differences at that time, but this principle has served as a guidepost to counsel others throughout the years. Now my major concern was to get well again.

After a month I heard both good news and bad news from the Arctic. The good news was that the military staff had delivered twenty barrels of surplus fuel oil to John and Helen's house. The bad news was that many of the people had backslidden and stopped coming to church. I decided to head for the Arctic quickly and continue my recuperation on the field.

I returned to Cambridge Bay to find that John and Helen had moved into their new house. Just before I had come down with hepatitis, we had purchased an old house for $300. With infinite patience, John took that building apart piece by piece, straightening the old nails, trying to salvage every bit of plywood and every foot of lumber, for in the high Arctic building materials are invaluable. John plodded along until finally he had a little two-bedroom house together. He had done a handsome job, and how pleased Helen was to have a home of her own.

Within a week the enlarged chapel was ready for services and the Eskimo people came out in full force. Many of them were restored to the Lord, others were saved, and in a couple of months the work of the Lord was once again progressing.

Springtime comes late in Cambridge Bay. On the Mackenzie River the ice begins going out by mid-June; but on Victoria Island it is late July before this happens. One summer it was unusually cold, with six-to-eight-foot drifts of snow that first week of July, and the ice on the lakes frozen solid. That year the ice never left the bay completely, with large floes shifting in and out. (The Eskimo language has more than one hundred words to describe types of snow, and almost as many for the various ice formations.)

Usually in late June we would walk to the lake five miles away to join the others at the fishing camp. We would fish together, visit in their tents, and when enough people gathered, we would have a service.

During the thawing process, the increased currents from shore water create dozens of six-inch to twenty-four-inch holes on these arctic lakes. The ice is still usually safe, and these holes are ideal for fishing.

We had been fishing for about five minutes one day when suddenly, without warning, the ice gave way under me. Frantically, I scrambled to grab the edges, for the very real danger is in being dragged down in the water and swept under the ice which was still about four feet thick. My muskrat parka and boots could be a deadly weight if they got soaked through. The ice kept breaking as I struggled to grab hold. Finally I grasped a piece that held me and clambered onto the ice, very wet.

I had no other clothes with me so there was only one thing to do: take off all the clothes that I could, wring them out, and stay inside the tent until I was reasonably dry. With only the heat from a primus stove, this took several hours. Then when I was partially dry, I went out to fish again.

Next day we picked our way another twelve miles across the tundra to where a few tents were scattered along the lakeshore, with char and trout hanging on racks to dry in the sun. I must have looked crazy toting a guitar along with my other gear over that rough terrain.

Hovak, a well-weathered old Eskimo woman, invited us into her tent where she had a blackened pot bubbling on the primus—duck soup, complete with a few feathers, head and feet sticking up. No matter, we ravenously devoured the potful. After a visit all around, and a little sing-song, back home across the tundra we went. How we welcomed every chance to minister the Word to any group we could!

In Cambridge Bay, later that summer, we were planning another building drive. We envisioned a Bible school in Cambridge Bay and therefore we would need additional space. Some used material was being shipped up from our church's campground in the south; yet I knew I was not well enough to tackle another building project. A young man from Seattle named David Freeman volunteered to come and build this new house, giving up his holidays plus taking time off without pay from his job.

Almost immediately David dug in, working long hours to construct this building. He was single and began to develop the idea that he would like to remain in the north as a missionary. The Eskimos were delighted. This would surely lead to matrimony, they thought—to them marriage is a very practical arrangement and one should not overlook all the fringe benefits.

So when David returned south the Eskimo people were quite disappointed. "Why didn't you go after that young man?" they demanded.

They had heard he was a pilot. "Just think—we could have gone polar bear hunting by plane!" they chided.

Helen Maksagak, one of the greatest northern matchmakers, finally said to me, "Well, that's it, Kayy, I give up. You're doomed to be single, because you want to be single."

During this building project I was so frustrated by my lack of energy that I came up with a self-diagnosis—laziness. With that firmly in mind, the big push was on. The building project continued. I was determined to beat this thing. Even though I still wasn't eating properly, I forced myself on, day after day. The result was that I was accomplishing little, yet becoming easily irritated.

However, there was a bright spot in sight. Iona was coming for a visit. She had left the nursing station in the Yukon and was coming to spend her holidays with me before starting the next job. I deeply respected and loved Iona and this feeling was mutual. She was my best friend. Eagerly, I clambered into the back of the pickup truck with a group of Eskimo Christians and drove out to the airport to welcome her.

Iona was used to my living in these pioneer circumstances. The gas lamp still dangled from the ceiling, but the rough bunk had been replaced by proper bunk beds that she had sent to me. The linoleum with the floral design was on the floor as usual, but there was also a sofa in the little kitchen-living room. This was another gift from Iona.

Best of all, in a few short weeks, an oil-burning cookstove would be installed. This meant we could dispense with the oil space heater and our trusty two-burner primus. For the first time in five years, I would have an oven, opening up a whole new world of food possibilities—baked goods, roasts, the luxuries of real bread, cakes, cookies and so on.

It had been nearly two-and-a-half years since I had seen Iona, so that night, with the long hours of daylight streaming through the windows we talked over the many experiences that had come our way. We laughed at many of the old happenings of the past and enjoyed a great time of Christian fellowship together. Finally, in the wee hours of the morning, we tucked into the bunk beds.

I quickly fell asleep, but Iona lay in her upper bunk wondering why so early in the evening I had drooped and wilted like a flower in the hot sun.

A few days later Iona spoke to me. "Kayy, something is drastically wrong with you. You're not yourself. I think you're relapsing with hepatitis."

My immediate reaction was, "Of course not! Nothing's wrong with me, I'm just lazy." She insisted that I have some tests, and they indicated that Iona was right. I rebelled, fighting the idea of bed rest violently.

Finally one evening, the crunch came. "Kayy," she said, "if you don't give up and go to bed, you have only one other alternative. In just a few weeks' time they'll take you out of here on a stretcher, fly you south and there you will probably spend at least six months in recuperation." I knew she was right. To bed I went.

Iona looked after me as though I were a princess. Soon the new oil range was installed and Iona prepared every kind of food in an effort to get me eating again. She even took it upon herself to order two hind quarters of beef at expensive air freight rates to be sure there would be sufficient protein in my diet.

After a few days of bed rest the change that came over me was unbelievable. Of course ten times a day I resisted this lying-down regimen. But after a couple of weeks of this treatment I felt as if a tent had lifted from me. I had been sick and was too stupid to realize it. Iona stayed on, not just a few weeks, but several months until she was convinced that I was completely recovered.

During this time no opportunity had opened up for Iona to nurse in Cambridge Bay, so she felt a time in the south would be a good refresher experience. Needless to say it was not a happy day for me when she flew out. After seeing her off at the airport at two o'clock on a cold, dark December morning, I returned to my little home and was temporarily overcome by its emptiness. I didn't like being tired, cold and all alone. But I dried my tears and decided the best thing to do was to get busy, so at three in the morning I plowed into preparations for the Christmas celebration just ahead.

As well, I had taken over the responsibility of postmistress which involved two afternoons a week. We were in the full swing of meetings—regular church services, boys' and girls' clubs and home visitation, plus five classes of religious instruction each week at the school. Keeping busy is always the best antidote for loneliness.

CHAPTER 20

An Eskimo Apostle Paul

The next spring John and I planned special meetings, inviting a stalwart of the faith, Paul Patkotak, to minister to our Cambridge Bay people. Paul was an outstanding Eskimo leader from Point Barrow. God's hand had been on his life in a remarkable way, even from childhood.

When only a youngster, Paul had wanted more education, but at that time there was no government aid for further education. Young Paul began trapping white foxes after school and on weekends, and at the end of two years he had saved enough money to go south. Still in his early teens, Paul secured passage on a freighter for Portland, Oregon, where he studied commercial subjects for the next six years.

When he was eighteen, in an Apostolic church in Portland, Paul was presented with the simple gospel and the clear claims of Christ upon his life. After hearing several people of various ethnic groups testify, Paul became convinced that this was for him. That evening he surrendered his life to Jesus Christ.

A tremendous change came over Paul. It was difficult for him to live for the Lord in the dorm, especially as he was the only Christian young person there. But he stood the test and after a few years returned to Alaska, a solid, spirit-filled Christian.

Paul was not ashamed of Christ and he freely shared his new-found faith with all his friends and relatives, but their response was very negative. They felt Paul had gone off the deep end and that he was mixed up in some wild, fanatical group. Instead of listening to his message, they ridiculed and scoffed him. Undaunted, Paul continued to pray and witness.

For over forty years this man stood for his convictions, often alone. He married an Eskimo girl and one evening, a short time afterward, as he knelt beside the bed to pray, the Holy Spirit began to convict Paul's wife. After the gas lamp was turned out, she began to sob uncontrollably.

"What's wrong?" Paul asked in alarm.

"I feel as if you're leaving me behind," she replied. Right in their little cabin Paul had the pleasure of leading his wife to the Lord Jesus Christ. Together they maintained a Christian home, rearing their five children in the ways of the Lord. Over the years God proved himself to be real to this brave Eskimo family who had stood so faithfully for Him. Paul's life was spared on different occasions and his prayers were often answered supernaturally.

One spring Paul and his cousin had been so successful on a caribou hunt, that they couldn't carry home all the meat. They had to cache some of the meat, piling the caribou and covering it with stones to keep the wolves and foxes from devouring it. Each man built his own cache in the same way, but before starting the long journey homeward, in the presence of his unbelieving cousin, Paul knelt before his cache. Lifting his hands towards heaven he asked God to protect his meat so that when he returned he would have a good supply to take home to his wife and children. His cousin mocked him for this; then they set out.

An Eskimo Apostle Paul

The time came when traveling again was possible and the men returned to collect their meat. The caches that had been identical when they left were not identical upon their return. The cousin's was in disarray, the rocks pushed aside, bones and remains of carcasses littering the ground.

Paul's was untouched. But circling his cache were many fresh tracks where wolves and foxes had paced round and round but somehow had not been able to touch Paul's meat. Again Paul dropped to his knees in the snow and praised the God who had shut the lions' mouths for Daniel of old, and who had now closed the mouths of the foxes and wolves. His cousin was shaken, and very soon he too trusted Paul's Lord and Savior.

At another time Paul and his family of four young children were camping for the winter on the barrens some sixty-five miles from town. One morning the children were crying, "Daddy, it's so long since we had any fruit. Please can we have fruit?" Paul assured them that if they prayed together, God would provide. After their usual morning devotions, Paul prepared to leave for his daily hunting trip. "Remember, God delights to give His children the desires of their heart," he reassured them.

As Paul traveled with his dog team, he felt a strong inclination to veer to the left although his plan was to head right. There was a high hill on the left and with spring approaching, the pulling was hard. Still Paul felt compelled to push on up the hill to the point where the dogs could no longer climb. Something glittering in the sun near the summit caught Paul's eye. Leaving the dogs, he hiked up the hill and there he pushed away the snow from the partly exposed shiny object—a large can. Although it was unmarked he knew it contained fruit.

Of course the contents were frozen but joyously Paul carried them home, thawed the can, and the delighted children had tinned fruit for supper. Can God furnish a table in the wilderness? Paul's family would never doubt that most assuredly He can.

For our special meetings in Cambridge Bay, Paul traveled

across the 1500 miles of arctic coastline via DEW line transport. As he stepped from the plane, what an impressive figure he made! Snowy white hair framing his strong, bronzed features, white eyebrows accentuating keen, twinkling eyes, a smile that swept a wave of kindness across his face—all in all a most distinguished gentleman, a leader in any crowd. His manner was never faltering but positive and decisive.

At seventy-three years, he was old for an Eskimo, yet unbelievably agile, with all his actions quick and steady. His hands never quivered, and for this he was grateful to God, because he had prayed for steadiness so that he could continue to earn his living as a fine carver specializing in intricate ivory bracelets and miniature figures. The people who once had mocked and scoffed him those forty long years now respected and honored him as a great man of faith in Eskimo land.

It was a pleasure and honor to have this godly man visit our community. Wherever Paul visited, everyone listened intently. Children stopped their playing and running around the house; trappers would pull off their fur parkas and mitts, and sit down to listen to the old man's stories. They all respected and loved him, from the youngest to the oldest. The church was packed every night, and a real deposit of faith and challenge was left in the hearts of the people.

CHAPTER 21

Arctic Ways of Life and Death

Helen Maksagak's youngest brother Jimmy had moved from the western Arctic to Cambridge Bay area, working on the DEW line, and, after a time, he came to live with John and Helen. Not long afterwards, he was attracted to a young Eskimo girl, Ann, and soon wedding bells were about to ring.

Because Jimmy was from the western Arctic he was more familiar with church weddings, and wanted the best. He took his bride down to the Hudson's Bay store and bought her the finest dress in the store. It was not a wedding dress, but just the same, she looked every inch a beautiful bride. Jimmy wore a nice suit, shirt and tie and appeared as Prince Charming himself.

Helen and I worked together to prepare an arctic-style reception: raisin bread, bannock, three or four frosted and decorated white cakes; tea, coffee and juice by the gallon. After everyone had wished the new couple God's blessing, they set off on their grand honeymoon back to John and Helen's house. But fancy clothes and elegant trimmings are not what really make a wedding beautiful.

Rather it's the awareness of God's presence, coupled with the beauty of love. Jimmy and Ann's love was deep and meaningful for they had discovered each other and each had made his own choice of a life partner.

This was quite contrary to the Eskimo custom of prearranged marriages which is on the way out. Traditionally, when a child was born it was then determined who that one would marry. Then, when the girl reached puberty, she was taken to the boy's home to be his wife on a permanent basis. If she didn't become pregnant, he might choose to send her home and take another wife. Love developed in these arranged marriages, and even if the wife did not become pregnant, the couple would often adopt children.

In the Arctic, the most unexpected things happen at weddings. Barry, a young Hudson's Bay clerk, had fallen in love with a very young Eskimo girl and they had asked if I would marry them. Neither were members of our church, but I was more than willing to help them set up their home honorably, in the fear of God and according to the laws of the country. The girl's father willingly signed the necessary consent forms for his daughter to be married. The date was set for the next Saturday.

In the meantime I had received a primary smallpox vaccination and the reaction was severe. I did not want to disappoint this young couple so I struggled out of bed to prepare for the wedding that evening.

At about a quarter to six we spotted a ship steaming around the inlet—the annual freight ship with tons of supplies for the Hudson's Bay store. This meant all hands had to be on deck probably around the clock.

Barry got a message from the Hudson's Bay manager. "Sorry you can't have the evening off, not even to get married," he was told. There was only one thing to do—hammer a big notice on the church door: "No wedding tonight because the freight ship has arrived." After nailing up this unusual message, I gratefully tumbled back into bed.

The next week, after the supplies had been unloaded and the ship departed (and the preacher recovered!), Barry and Adelaide were married. This time it was Adelaide's turn to break with tradition as she came down the aisle, a beautiful bride in a lovely white pantsuit. About six weeks later, both Barry and Adelaide were wonderfully saved. Thus, another Christian home was established.

One area of Eskimo social life that, to my mind, has been greatly misunderstood is the marriage relationship. In our southern society, it seems to be the general consensus of opinion that the Eskimo man is very free to give his wife away to anyone who comes to the door.

It is true that there have been times when the Eskimo has given his wife in return for remuneration of one description or an other. But I have found that this is by no means the rule of the day. Most Eskimo couples love each other just as intensely as couples do anywhere else in the world, and because they love each other, they are jealous of each other. Many times Eskimo women, Christian or otherwise, have come to me heartbroken because their husbands have gone off with other women.

In a remote arctic village I knew of a Catholic woman whose heart sank when she discovered her husband had been unfaithful. In total despair she headed for the ocean to take her life. But on the way, she heard strains of happy music coming from a little building. Thinking she had nothing to lose, this heartsick, desperate woman dropped in for just a few minutes. She was gripped by the gospel singing and message, and instead of drowning herself in the ocean, made her way to the altar. The heavy burden was lifted and a deep sense of love and forgiveness was born in her heart towards her unfaithful husband.

A short time later, he said to her, "I'm not fit to be your husband after hurting you so deeply." He wept as he spoke to her and it wasn't long until he too made his way to the altar. Today that home is beautifully reunited and radiantly happy.

One thing that has radically upset the Eskimo husband-wife

relationship is the tremendous drinking problem. The parties often extend into all-night orgies. At these times there is much husband and wife swapping, and, as a result, a tremendous rise in the V.D. rate.

It used to be an accepted way of life for a single girl to have a baby before marriage to prove she could produce a child. Trial marriages were very common and in some areas still are. But with more education available, and with new career opportunities developing, the young Eskimo women today often prefer not to become pregnant too early in life.

There still is often no real shame attached to bearing a child before marriage, except of course in the Christian community where the moral standard is raised. But on the whole, children born outside of wedlock are very quickly accepted into the homes. The mother and father of the girl who has given birth to the child will very often adopt this little one. Grandma is never without babies, it seems.

No difference is made in most instances, and even if the child happens to be blond and blue-eyed, it is very much accepted. In fact, I recall overhearing two Eskimo girls in an argument about this.

"Ai!" the one girl taunted. "You can't produce a blue-eyed, blond baby like I did. You don't know how!"—and that was the crowning insult.

Not only was I in the Arctic to share in their joys, but also in their sorrows. Death is a dreaded event, no matter in what part of the world we live. In the Eskimo community, where the home and family are very close units, the pangs of death cut deeply into the Eskimo heart.

About six o'clock one morning, my kitchen door suddenly burst open with David, a young Eskimo father, crying, *"Paniea tokoyok, tokoyok!* My daughter is dead, she is dead!"* Fortunately, I was up early that summer morning and was just having breakfast. I jumped quickly on my little Honda and sped off to Dave and Lena's home where their pitiful baby was lying motionless on the bed. The little mother was gently stroking her dead baby's feet, caressing the little body that had died so suddenly during the night. The child had been sleeping with the parents and had smothered to death. David was unable to arouse the baby and, in desperation, had come to me.

When the police truck drove up, I gently wrapped the little body in a blanket and took it to the nursing station, then returned to comfort the family who were in tears of sorrow for their great loss. After we prayed together, Lena took on a new strength and immediately asked about funeral arrangements.

"Could we have the funeral tonight?" Lena wanted to know.

Eskimo custom is that the sooner the service can be conducted for a departed one, the better. They feel that the spirit doesn't really rest until the body has been committed to the grave. This was rather a tall order. The local village carpenter would first have to build a small plywood box that would serve as a casket. But it was summertime, with long hours of daylight, so I assured Lena I would do everything in my power to have a funeral service that evening.

In the north, often the preacher has to double as undertaker. Lena brought in new clothes and asked if I would dress the baby. Then we placed the little body in the box covered with white canvas and put a few artificial flowers on top. The Eskimo people appreciated the extras of covering the bare box and putting flowers on the casket, which was not always done by the other churches, but I felt it added a little warmth to a very sad occasion.

The funeral service was set for eight o'clock that same evening. The town was shocked by this death and the church was crowded. Lena was from a large family, many of whom had married and had children of their own, and of course they were all in attendance. At the end of the service I asked the parents to come up and carry the casket out. This is also an Eskimo custom. They like to participate in some part of the funeral service; in that way they are able to lend a helping hand to the one they have lost.

I shall never forget that tender moment. David knelt beside his little daughter's casket and first prayed. This was most unusual, and it turned out to be David's first step in turning to Jesus Christ.

We proceeded up the long trail to the hill where we buried the dead. The men had been working all day, digging down just a couple of feet through the rocks, preparing a grave to lay this little one in. Then as we gathered around the graveside, the men slowly lowered the little flowered box into the rough-looking grave with stones sticking out on all sides.

It's always heartrending, but this time the Eskimos were especially moved and so was I. It seemed so hard to commit this beautiful, little baby to this rough, jagged grave. After returning from the graveyard in the government trucks, I invited the family in for a cup of tea and a little time together, hoping to further comfort their troubled hearts.

The Eskimo people always seemed exceptionally appreciative and grateful that I serve them in this sad area of their lives, regardless of their religious background. Sometimes I bury people whom I have never seen, people from other villages who die in the hospital at Cambridge Bay. Often they are little babies who die from respiratory disorders; sometimes it is the aged.

The week after burying David and Lena's little baby, several members of the family were in church. What a joy it was to see Lena and David both come forward and accept Christ, their lives wonderfully touched by the gospel!

In the next service, Lena's teenage sister, Gwen, and her boyfriend came and gave their hearts to Christ. Gwen had not understood the gospel and had been very outspoken in her anti-Christian views. But, oh, the change in this teenager when she, too, was converted! Soon the mother was saved, and later on so was Lena's father, old Angulalik, a colorful trader of the north.

One by one, David and Lena's families took their stand for Jesus Christ. Tremendous changes took place in their lives. The drinking problems were gone, the old night life was finished as they became new creatures in Jesus Christ and found the joy that Christ alone can bring. It was indeed a touching scene when Lena stood up to testify, thanking God for saving her and then said: "My baby is taking me to heaven. Now I am saved and I will meet my baby again."

Some time later, a couple burst through my doorway, crying and wailing as the Eskimos do at the death of a loved one. Their reaction to sorrow is very normal, and usually after prayer they cease crying. To the outsider it seems that they philosophically accept their loss as fate, but in actuality they suffer intensely and have a deep sense of sorrow over the loss of their loved ones.

This Saturday morning, the couple came in and told me their story. Their son John had died out on the tundra after eating contaminated meat. It had been an unusually warm summer. His cache of meat was well under ground in the permafrost, but because of the warmth of the summer, the sun's heat had penetrated to the meat and contaminated it. After his death, the R.C.M.P. had sent his body south for an autopsy.

Now it had just been returned, and Terry, the young Anglican minister, was going to conduct John's funeral. The body that had now been deceased fourteen days without embalming, was in a box in Terry's church, waiting for the service that afternoon. Terry was a new minister, a fine, dedicated young man, but not too familiar with the Eskimo custom that they must see, touch and in many instances, kiss the body, so they can fully accept the fact that the person is dead. Terry didn't want to open that box, because he knew the body would be in bad shape. So the Eskimo family, in desperation, asked if I could explain their custom to the minister and have him open the casket for them to see their loved one before the funeral service.

Terry was obliging. "All right, Kayy. I'll open the box, but you go with them. You understand their customs better than I."

So I went over with the couple and when we lifted the lid, there was John, his face black, a terrible stench coming from his corpse. After a few minutes with the body, the couple left. I returned home, only to have more and more relatives come to me and ask, "Please, can we see John?" Again I would phone Terry and he would say, "O.K., but you take them."

After the service that afternoon, I bounced along on my Honda, following the government pickup truck that served as a hearse. It carried the casket to its resting place on the hill a mile from town. There it rested, and rested and rested, for two months, along with half a dozen other caskets no one had bothered to bury. Finally, after several phone calls, a crew was sent up to dig shallow graves and lay the bodies to a decent rest. This little oversight was all too frequent.

CHAPTER 22

Ruth and Nels

One day, very unexpectedly, Helen Maksagak asked if she could come to see me "about some very special business." I knew that she and John were having a real struggle supporting their six children and themselves. Although they had come to work for us in the mission, we encouraged our native workers to provide their own support, and John was doing this with odd jobs.

Helen had just received her family allowance and they desperately needed this to make ends meet. She came in that day with some money in her hand and eagerly thrust it towards me.

"Kayy, this is my tithe from the family allowance," she said, with a glowing face.

I found it difficult to accept this money and yet knew she was being obedient to God's Word. With what little she had, she was honoring God. Helen needed that money. She could certainly put it to good use for food and clothing for the children, but she must honor her Lord first.

"God bless you, Helen. He will reward you!" was all I could

say. That touching incident remained in my heart, and some time later while visiting Inuvik in the western Arctic, I shared the story of Helen's faithfulness in honoring God with her tithe even in difficult times. This so stirred many of the Eskimo workingmen that they caught up with their past tithing.

God did honor Helen and in a short time John had a steady job. Later on he was selected to represent his people at various meetings with our government. God blessed them in their home. They moved to a government house and then to a larger three-bedroom home. They gave up everything for God, but God is no man's debtor. He returns a hundredfold, in this life and in the next.

At about the same time, the school principal was looking for houseparents to care for the children from outlying areas who had to come into Cambridge Bay for school. (Not all the children were sent on to Inuvik.) They had to be steady people, not overcome with the problems of drunkenness, gambling and so on. Would I know such a couple?

Immediately, my mind flashed back to Nels and Ruth Pulk in Inuvik, who certainly would be top quality houseparents. And they had only two children. Immediately, I contacted them. Yes, they would be quite happy to come. Nels was willing to leave his good job and Ruth was willing to leave their very modern apartment.

Apparently another minister in town expressed his strong disapproval to the Catholic priest about the idea of a Pentecostal family taking over the school hostel. Said the priest to the minister: "Do *you* have a stable couple in your church with a small family who could do the job?"

"Well, no," he admitted.

"I don't have any either, so I think we both should shut up," the priest concluded.

Helen was so pleased to know that her sister Ruth would live nearby. Nels and Ruth became houseparents and the children loved them. They accepted the children as their own. It was a very happy home situation for children who were away from their own homes ten long months of the year. The children so appreciated Ruth and

Nels that they insisted on following them to church services and Sunday school.

The parents out in the camps were delighted that the children were so happy with the Pulks, and that they were attending Sunday school. Many of those children's lives were touched with the gospel and some made lasting decisions for Christ. God met them in a way that they will never be able to forget. And they in turn took the message back to their homes in outlying camps.

Ruth was an outstanding Eskimo lady. I remember the first time I met her at Reindeer Station. After five years of hospitalization in Edmonton with a severe case of tuberculosis, Ruth had just returned to the Arctic to take her place again among the Inuit. She was a very striking girl with a lot of ability and grace.

As I watched her in Cambridge Bay, I couldn't help but think Nels had chosen for himself a beautiful wife and a godly woman. Ruth has been a real helpmeet to him in every way.

She became my closest friend in the Arctic. I could pop into her house at any time and know that I was totally welcome. This helped me over some difficult days.

Ruth and Nels spent several years with us in Cambridge Bay and were a very strong testimony for the Lord by the lives they lived, and the work they did in the hostel and in the church. Ruth became an excellent song leader and Nels displayed his musical talents by being our chief guitarist.

One weekend in February, Nels decided to take his son, Mike, along with an Eskimo boy from the hostel for a caribou hunt. They traveled by snowmobile to a lake about forty-five miles from Cambridge Bay, set up the tent, and then Nels left to take a quick run looking for caribou tracks.

A white-out came down and Nels couldn't find his way back to the tent. Round and round he circled, desperately, and then, to his dismay, the snowmobile kicked over and died. Out of gas!

Nel could catch glimpses of the high tower at Cambridge Bay so he felt he could find his way back to the village. About three o'clock Saturday afternoon this hardy reindeer herder set out across the crusted snow, arriving at Cambridge Bay close to midnight. The weather had cleared somewhat, and with an Eskimo R.C.M.P. constable, immediately Nels rushed back to where he had left the boys camped.

Meanwhile, when Nels had not returned, the boys concluded he had run out of gas, so they set out with the two-gallon can of gas, following Nels's snowmobile tracks. Dick was thirteen; Mike was a mere ten. Finally they realized that they too had lost their way.

Carefully, young Dick, drawing on the centuries of arctic survival techniques born into every Eskimo, dug away the snow by a rock and made a shelter for Mike to sleep. All through the night Dick kept vigil, moving Mike every couple of hours, carefully keeping his face covered. In the morning they began to walk, back and forth across the big lake as they had been taught. The boys had a package of Kool-Aid and this, mixed with snow, was their only nourishment. Both committed Christians, these two boys were praying for rescue as they plodded through the storm.

When Nels and the constable reached the tent, to their dismay there was not a trace of the boys! Nels fell on the caribou skins of the empty tent, beseeching God to have mercy. Late Sunday night they returned to Cambridge Bay. Nels and Ruth were distraught. Throughout the night, the Christians rallied round, crying out to God for these two boys lost on the bleak barrens in 45 below weather for more than twenty-four hours.

Very early in the morning, Helen and I went through the settlement, rousing up those with snowmobiles to help in the search, and at 5:30 there was a roar as they headed out across the frozen wilderness. All morning they searched. The white-out had cleared, but they could find no tracks.

At noon a search plane was brought in with Willie Lazerick, a very fine veteran bush pilot, at the controls. Just as darkness was closing in on this third day, Willie spotted two small figures and swooped down on the lake.

Back at the hostel the telephone rang and I answered. "We've heard from Willie Lazerick. He has the boys!" I exclaimed.

A great shout went up from all the Christians gathered there with Ruth. "Praise the Lord!" Immediately on arrival back at the village the boys were rushed to the doctor. Forty-eight hours without food and shelter in low degree weather—surely the damage must be extensive. The doctor shook his head incredulously. They were unharmed. Five minutes later, Mike and Dick were on their way to the Hudson's Bay to fill up on pop and chocolate bars. They were now the heroes of the town.

The men returned on their snowmobiles and what a time of rejoicing there was! Not only had the lost been found, but they had been miraculously protected from all frostbite and harm.

CHAPTER 23

Iona's Vision

As the old pickup truck rattled up to the post office door and dropped off two sacks of mail, I had no premonition that for me it held unexpected but delightful news. After a year of nursing in the south, Iona had decided that she would like to return to the Arctic. There was an opening in Cambridge Bay for a nurse and she had accepted the position.

Iona came to live with me in the second mission house where things were much more modern and convenient. Together we luxuriated in what seemed to us such spacious living quarters, all 512 square feet!

The government had approved a plan of low cost housing for arctic residents, and some of these units were being built in Cambridge Bay. The first houses were twelve-by-twenty-four-foot "matchboxes," but compared to the shacks that the Eskimos had been living in, they were a big improvement.

Each year the houses seemed to be just a little bigger and better. From one bedroom houses in the beginning, the government approved three and even four bedroom houses in most Eskimo villages.

Next came electricity, a luxury already available in the white people's homes. I have always believed that missionaries should not live on a standard above the people to whom they are ministering, but at the same time they should keep abreast with the increased standard of living. Consequently I sent a letter to Vancouver asking for $200 to hook up our one bedroom home. This had to be done quickly as the contractor was in town for only a few weeks. A qualified electrician would probably not be in Cambridge Bay for a whole year. One evening Iona came home very embarrassed. The only radio-telephone in town was at the nursing station and a wire had come through for me from Vancouver. The other nurse had turned to Iona puzzled. "I think this message must be coded!" she said. The word from the head office read: "Since installation is more than $100 suggest return to gas lamps."

The only thing to do was to find other means of supplying the need, so I took a temporary job preparing the noon lunch at the school. The face of the Arctic was changing rapidly, but it is difficult for a head office three thousand miles away to understand what's taking place on the mission field. One has to be at the scene of action to fully appreciate it.

After only a year-and-a-half, Iona was forced to go south because of failing health. A biopsy confirmed that she was suffering from incurable cancer. Surgery was not indicated. Nothing could be done other than radiation treatments.

I phoned the Vancouver office and Pastor Layzell very kindly gave me a leave of absence, providing I could find someone to take over the mission station during my absence. Another woman preacher, Eva Nichol, graciously abandoned her holiday plans and flew into the north to relieve me.

The Eskimo people were shaken by the news of Iona's cancer, but their faith was unwavering. After all, hadn't God done the miraculous for them in the past and answered their prayers? Hadn't He healed Kailek? Hadn't He stopped Eva's hemorrhage? Hadn't He done many miracles? They confidently expected Iona to be healed. They prayed earnestly and they fervently believed this would happen.

I spent the next six months with Iona, and in the last few days of her life, she asked for a pen and paper to write a final letter to the northland, encouraging the Eskimo people to serve God, and to be faithful. And then Iona enclosed a check as her final tithe. This deeply impressed the church at Cambridge Bay and it certainly helped many of them to not forget the Lord's tithe.

Before she passed away, Iona made sure all her business affairs were in order, leaving some funds to the church and some funds for her burial.

"Bury me cheaply and keep the change," she told me with a brave grin. She also gave to me personally her $5,000 death benefit. "Tuck it away for your old age," Iona requested, but I told her there was no way I could do that. "I'll build something to your memory in the Arctic," I promised.

As I stood by her bedside that evening of December 4, 1966, I realized she was not going to be with us much longer. The doctor had told me it would be a very hard death, that she would literally drown in the fluid in her lungs. But contrary to expectations, Iona regained consciousness and then, as it were, she went to sleep. She died as she had lived, with great peace.

The news of her death was a great shock to the Eskimo people, for they had fully expected that she would live and return to their land. It was also a blow to me personally, but we can't understand all the ways of God. Many things we must accept by faith.

Very shortly after her death, I returned to the north, to the people who had become my people. I felt they needed me, and I knew that I needed them. It was a difficult year for me personally as I struggled to overcome the aching sense of loss. It was the only year in the Arctic that I was aware of the absence of the sun, oppressed by the constant darkness—the only time I ever felt that the long winter night would never come to an end. What a joy it was to see the sun return! During those days the Christian Eskimos were very understanding and compassionate, and I will always remember how they ministered to me as I endeavored to comfort them too. Iona's vision had always been that we should build a new church in Cambridge Bay. The last year of her life she told me repeatedly: "Kayy, you're going to need a bigger church, a better one, with a good apartment overhead. Everything is changing in the north. The pioneer days in these villages will soon be over and you need to be one step ahead if you are to win the people."

Personally, I had had enough building. I knew the struggles and I really didn't want to start again. "But that $5,000 gift, Lord. Is that what you want me to do with it?" I prayed.

The next year a million-dollar school was going up in Cambridge Bay. I made it my business to go over and meet the superintendent. We struck up quite a good relationship, and I shared with him my desire to build a new chapel.

"Could we have first choice of any surplus material left on site at the completion of this large construction project?" I asked. He was most helpful and did arrange for me to secure a great deal of material at less than cost.

We were short on one of item—two-by-six foot lumber. As I walked by the construction site one day, the boss was very upset. "That stupid outfit in Edmonton!" he fumed. "They've short-ordered us on two-by-fours and sent a double lot of two-by-sixes!" He was startled when I laughed.

"The Lord hath need of them," I told him. And the Lord's house got them!

Now that we had most of the material together, how were we to go about it? A two-story building is a big project, bigger than anything I'd tackled so far. We needed skilled help with this. One day I had an inspiration. A new construction company had just come to town to erect a couple of buildings. I wondered if they

180

would like me to supply meals for the crew. This idea tickled the superintendent and I found myself landing a job that was to begin the next morning at six o'clock.

Quickly we cleared out a back room, converting it to a little dining area, and made a separate entrance so that the men could go in and out without being in our home. Even though we had no running water, we were in the restaurant business!

Marian Page, a qualified public health nurse whom I had met in the south while I was nursing Iona, had joined me that year. Now this new project had come up. Neither of us had much experience at cooking, but Marian was willing to try. So often when we ask the Lord for help, He turns to us and says, "What is that in thine hand?" For me, it was a frying pan; for Marian, a rolling pin, as she whipped up dozens of scrumptious pies.

Call it devious, or simply seizing the opportunity—my plan, once we had these skilled workmen eating at our table, was to hire them to do the main construction on our new church. If the foundations were well laid and the building well framed, we figured we could cope with finishing off the interior ourselves.

Marian and I decided that all the profits from our catering venture would go to the building fund for the new church. In fear and trembling we arose that first morning to prepare our first meal. To our pleasant surprise we found that they were quite easy to please. It wasn't going to be nearly as difficult as we had anticipated.

But the hours were demanding. We had to be up at five o'clock in the morning. We were often going until midnight with our missionary work and the post office, which was open three afternoons a week in a little room behind the dining room.

When the mail came in, we would sort it immediately, because soon the whole town would be at the door, even if it was 2 A.M.! The twenty bags of sorted mail would evaporate in minutes.

Room and board is hard to come by in these small arctic villages. At that time there were no hotels, and few homes open to take people in. So I wasn't surprised when the construction boss called me the next year and asked, "You going to be in business again, Kayy?"

To double our earnings, in addition to serving meals we decided to put up a bunkhouse before attempting a church. "Two rules, fellas," I told them. "No liquor and no women. And no second chances! Break either rule and you leave!"

The second night they decided to test me. Someone had been drinking in the bunkhouse and I found out. Quietly but firmly I asked him to leave. The next day, this chap came back and very meekly asked, "Do you suppose there is any way I can get a meal?"

I looked at him, and with a smile I gave in. "Even bad boys have to eat. Come on into the dining room," I answered. But he didn't sleep in the bunkhouse again. So they learned that I could be as tough as a boiled owl about the rules.

We also catered meals for the commissioner's party in our little dining room, and then later in the apartment over the church. The judicial party, in their swing through the north, ate at our place as did the governor-general's press party, nineteen of them. Always the comments were superlative. "The best apple pie in the north!" Commissioner Hodgson complimented Marian.

Then one of the helicopter pilots with a survey crew seemed to be going out of his way to be extra helpful to me. One day I remarked I would like some aerial photos of Cambridge Bay.

"Kayy, I'll take you up in the helicopter." It never occurred to me that he meant right then. After all, it was 35 below. But only minutes later, there was his chopper setting down in the yard.

"Get your camera, Kayy," he called.

"I'm coming too," Marian yelled. As we scrambled aboard, his face fell somewhat but he was game and set out to get me the best shots anybody ever had of Cambridge Bay. Trouble was, I had no film in my camera, but only I knew that.

"How about that, Kayy?" he'd call.

"Great, just great," I would answer.

"Let's tip it another ten degrees." He hovered and dipped and just about stood on his head for me. I was carefully counting my camera clicks not to go beyond twenty. When we got back he told all the boys, "Kayy sure got some great shots, eh Kayy?"

"Wonderful views," I agreed. I just hoped he would have moved on to the next job before the time elapsed when my "roll of film" should have been developed!

Maybe I got paid back for the evil of my ways, because the company he worked for went broke and never paid us the $1,500 board bill they owed us!

One day I had a phone call. "Kayy, could you handle another twenty-two men?" A crew was coming to town en route farther north. They would be in Cambridge Bay for two days, supposedly. But this was the Arctic. The weather closed in, the winds blew, the storms raged and the men were there for nearly two weeks. Well, when you're feeding five, what's another twenty-two? Cooking for that crowd on one small oil range without the aid of running water did present some rather gigantic problems, but we managed with two sittings at each meal.

With the funds coming in nicely from this hectic catering business there would be no problem paying workmen to start the new chapel. The days and weeks passed. All the additional building supplies ordered from the south arrived.

There was just one hitch: the construction men were too busy to start on the church. July and August passed, September came, and finally, about the nineteenth of September, the carpenter said to me, "Now I have time. Tomorrow I can begin to build that church." But this was unseasonably late in the year at Cambridge Bay to begin such a large project. It could be disastrous if we didn't get the building closed in and the roof on. A lot of material was involved and it sounded very foolhardy.

I got on my little red Honda and headed down the winding gravel road towards the river to pray and meditate about this. Was it foolhardy, or should we act in faith? The weather had been dismal and overcast for days and the wind was blowing, normal weather for this time of year. Everything seemed dreary and there was nothing to encourage the launching of a large building project.

I put out a fleece to the Lord and said, "Lord, you know it's late in the season. Any veteran northerner would say it's ridiculous to start a two-story building the twentieth of September. But Lord, if this is your will and if you really want us to build then let tomorrow be a very bright, warm, sunny day, without wind."

I had firmly decided that if the weather was still dismal and dreary, it would be no go.

Next morning I wakened to bright sunlight streaming in the windows! "Good, Lord, there's the sun," I shouted. "But how about the wind?" The fall of the year is known to be a windy time, with the winds blowing almost continuously in the Cambridge Bay area. In fact, it's almost a freak when there is no wind for a day or two. I opened the door and stepped outside. There wasn't a wind from any direction! "Thank you, Jesus!" I knew, even though it seemed contrary to human reasoning, we had the go ahead on the building.

The carpenters moved in, and in just a few days the floor was laid. In another few days the lower structure framework was up. By the end of September the roof was on, and we hired a crew of Eskimo workers to close the building in.

The Christian men rallied behind this project by working in the evenings. It was quite a sight one night when they were framing the walls. The carpenter had worked all day on his own project and then came over to be foreman for our Eskimo crew. We rigged up a bank of lights with floods borrowed from the DEW line and any other sizable lights we could find in town. Until two or three in the morning the ring of hammers was heard throughout the village. The church was going up! Nels Pulk especially gave days and days of his time to get that building closed in.

When the winter did come it was hard slugging. Often the men would have to come in to warm up, and then go back out again. In between cooking the meals, Marian, Ruth Pulk and I worked along with the men, putting on the aluminum siding. It was very cold, but so rewarding to see the building getting finished. Yet there was still a massive job to be done finishing the interior.

I phoned Vancouver explaining to them that we were just about exhausted from this long cooking project as well as the normal missionary work, and the post office. Pastor Layzell suggested that two men come in to help us finish the inside of the chapel—Lou Peterson, the assistant pastor at Glad Tidings Temple in Vancouver and Dave Freeman. Pastor Peterson could stay on and dedicate the new church.

Finally the date was set for our D-day, November 18. And what a great day it was, a time of real excitement in the village! Everybody came to the dedication of this new building that had just sprung up so late in the fall—the Eskimos, many of the village whites and DEW line personnel. Even though that night the twenty-four-by-sixty-foot chapel was already jam-packed, what a joy it was to have more space!

The chapel was really quite handsome with wood-paneled walls, acoustic-tile ceiling with large stained beams, and new beige tile floor (this time we didn't get nearly so much guck on top of the tiles!).

We didn't have our pews yet so we brought in benches from the old chapel and borrowed chairs from the school. On the red-carpeted platform, Nels Pulk and Joseph Otokiak provided the music with two electric guitars. (The organ came later.)

It was a tremendous sense of fulfilment for me personally to see the vision of my co-worker become a reality. This was Iona's final contribution to the Inuit of the north. We printed programs for the dedication service with a large photo of Iona on the cover. For months, even years afterwards, I saw these pictures hanging on the walls in Eskimo homes.

All of us seemed to be in a state of total exhaustion after the big push to get the church ready for dedication day. But it was with rejoicing hearts that we tumbled into bed that night, again realizing the tremendous faithfulness of our God. And our catering business had paid off quite handsomely. At the end of three years, this new building valued at $85,000 was debt free.

As the months passed, several of the Christian Eskimos became very interested in water baptism. After reading the Scripture about Paul being baptized, Leonie phoned me. "Why can't we be baptized just like in Bible days?" And so we found ourselves preparing for water baptism, the first service of its kind in Cambridge Bay.

We decided to build a collapsible baptismal tank, a plywood box with vinyl swimming pool liner ordered from Eaton's in Vancouver. When it came to figuring out stress and displacement, I was wishing I'd paid closer attention in physics class. How much pressure could the vinyl liner take? Then add the weight of the native elder, myself and the one to be baptized. "Well, Lord, just hold it all together for us," I prayed as Tommy and I finished the task, and ordered the water truck to empty 400 icy gallons into the tank.

The Eskimos were flabbergasted. "What are you going to do with this big tub, Kayy? Are you all going to have a bath together?"

How in the world were we ever going to heat the water? We decided to bring down tubs of hot water from the apartment upstairs. But that raised the water level even more.

We had special water baptismal classes, explaining the doctrine clearly from the Scriptures to the sixteen candidates. On the scheduled day, a blizzard howled through the village, with the wind chill factor dipping temperatures to 85 degrees below. Surely we shouldn't have people baptized and then go out into that storm! I phoned around and the response was unanimous. "Put it off? Nothing doing!" It seemed that the whole village came out to witness the first baptism in Cambridge Bay.

John Maksagak, Pastor David Heubert from Chilliwack, British Columbia, and I all climbed into the oversized tank, and one by one the candidates stepped into the very cold water. Very quickly my legs became numb, but the sixteen Eskimos who followed their Lord that night in waters of baptism didn't even seem to notice the cold.

Each one in turn stood in the icy water and testified joyously, "I'm so glad the Lord has saved my soul and I want to go all the way with Him." Then they dripped their way upstairs where we had partitioned off two areas as dressing rooms for the men and women.

The other Eskimo Christians now had seen what it was like to be baptized and many more indicated their desire to follow their Lord. And so the baptismal tank remained in place for a week. Night after night we climbed into that tank to baptize more believers. They believed that as they identified with Christ in this symbol of His death and burial that they too would rise up in new strength, to serve the Lord in newness of life. How they rejoiced as they came up from the waters!

One woman who was baptized was disappointed because one area of her face was not covered by water. This seemed to rob her of the blessing of having followed her Lord totally. I encouraged her that it was really an act of faith, and that she accept it by faith, but to her it was a problem. So we arranged that she was to come down again early Saturday morning.

This time as we baptized her, I was sure that we were pushing her almost to the bottom of the tank. She came up happy and joyful. She now had fully followed her Lord. That was Leonie, who had to have it done right, and who has gone on to be one of our choicest trophies of the gospel.

CHAPTER 24

Alcohol—a Major Problem

Marian Page became my quiet, unruffled co-worker in the church and the post office, and a great sounding board for me personally, often giving very wise counsel.

After several years of working with boys' and girls' clubs, home visitation and the teaching ministry, Marian decided she could make an even bigger contribution in Eskimo land by returning to the nursing profession. She was able to secure a position as public health nurse in Cambridge Bay where she still serves the people.

A nurse's life in the Arctic is certainly not her own. At any time she may be called out for an emergency flight. Often the phone rings in the middle of the night, calling for a nurse escort for such a flight.

Marian was often responding to emergency calls. One such case involved a very sick baby in the village of Gjoa Haven. Visibility was practically nil for landing, but it was literally a matter of life or death. With immense skill, the pilot set the plane down. They picked up the little child and headed for Yellowknife and the hospital.

The baby was dreadfully ill. Aboard the Twin Otter, Marian improvised a tube to suck the congestion from the baby's throat. Head winds made the flight considerably longer than normal, but finally they saw the lights of Yellowknife, landed and rushed the baby to the hospital. Fortunately the baby lived. Over coffee, the engineer confided to Marian that the winds had eaten up the fuel and there was nowhere along the way where they could take on more. So they'd landed on empty tanks. "We flew in on fumes and a prayer!" he had to conclude.

Unfortunately, much of the nurses' work in the Arctic is caused by the abuse of liquor, and without question, liquor has become the major problem of the north. In Cambridge Bay the whites decided that the only way to handle this drinking problem was to teach the Eskimos how to drink. If liquor is always available, they reasoned, then the Eskimo would learn to be moderate in his drinking. A beer outlet was opened at the Hudson's Bay store and flown in by the plane load.

So what happened? The more liquor available, the greater the problems for the Inuit. The violence involved in the drinking parties in the north is beyond belief. One Eskimo, Luke, under the influence of liquor became so violent that he took a hammer and literally beat in the skull of another man. The victim had to be flown out on a charter plane to Yellowknife and then on to Edmonton. Fortunately, he lived but it left him with a serious speech impediment. This wasn't Luke's first or only time with a hammer. More instances occurred later.

Black eyes were the order of the day after a night of drinking. The Eskimo women often worked with dark glasses on even in winter because of the severe beatings they received during the night parties. It became a common occurrence for someone to stumble into my door in the early hours of the morning looking for refuge from the violent storms caused by drinking. Often they would come in beaten up, bleeding and drunk. After talking with them, listening to them, and filling them as full of black coffee as I could, I would put them to bed on the carpet for the night. Sometimes they would stay a day or two. When the beer outlet was open, my living room floor was often crowded with terrified children and women fearing for their lives.

The wild fear expressed on the faces of little children reveals the great insecurity they feel when their parents have these fights. Sometimes the little ones come running to me in the dead of winter, late at night, crying, "Kayy, quickly! My dad is pounding mom and I think he is gonna kill her."

It was a strange thing, but every time I would step into a drunken brawl, as soon as the Eskimos recognized my parka and knew who I was, they would immediately stop fighting. I could walk into the middle of a fight and they would put their hands down, saying, "Sorry, Kayy Gordon. Sorry, can't help it."

When the Eskimo hunters and trappers got the taste of alcohol and became involved in all-night orgies, even their dog teams suffered. The plight of the Eskimo dogs was always pitiful. It was a great day when the snowmobile came to the country and it has now practically replaced the dog teams. If ever dogs lived a dog's life, it was in the north. And when their master got drunk, the dogs' needs were completely forgotten.

Often dog teams are staked along the beach. As the tide rises, the procedure is to move the dog team higher up on the beach, away from the water level. One springtime, a trapper was drinking. He left his dog team on the beach. An all-night poker game was in session and the frightened barking of the dogs didn't reach his ears. All through that night the dogs yelped and cried—and then there was complete silence. In the morning I went down to the shore, and there to my horror lay the whole team drowned while they were tied to the stake.

It was a deplorable sight to see even young children under the influence of liquor and beer. After the parents would drink themselves into a state of unconsciousness, the kids would experiment with these beverages that their parents couldn't seem to live without. Alcohol had become more important to many adults than food or clothing. The young kids would imbibe the cans of beer and polish off the bottles left on the table. I know of one couple who decided their three-year-old son should learn how to drink, and it became the joke of the evening to give little Willy a can of beer and let him drink until he started to stagger.

School attendance was radically affected by the drinking problem. Teachers would be in despair because the children were home sleeping. Or if they did go to school, they quickly fell asleep at their desks. They had been up all night, trying to look after their parents.

When the children couldn't cope any longer with the drinking situation in the home they would wander through the streets, visiting homes until the situation there became too bad. Then they would often come to some of the Christian Eskimos for a place to sleep where they could feel safe and secure.

It was a common sight to see several children, with no place to go, sleeping on the floor in Christian homes. Many, many children have run to my home in the middle of the night—often without parkas and without mitts, shaking not only from the cold, but also from fear.

"My dad is going to kill my mom. Please help us," they would cry. "We can't sleep in our house, we're afraid." This is the plight of so many Eskimo children. The terrified expressions on their little faces would reveal the awful evils of liquor to anyone.

Basically because a few white people selfishly want the privilege of having subsidized beer available for their own use, it is deplorable that this great burden was placed upon the Cambridge Bay Eskimo in the midst of a tremendous social transition. They are struggling to cope with all the changes in their land and culture, and we have placed on them the additional problems created by liquor. This is the greatest disservice, the most grave injustice ever done to our native people.

Alcohol—a Major Problem

The full story of the wreckage of human lives has not yet been told in the Arctic. The younger generation is reaping a terrible harvest from this injustice.

A beautiful young girl was missing from the village one night. Everybody was so drunk in her family that no one wondered where Topsie might be. The next morning, an Eskimo woman on her way to the Hudson's Bay store stumbled over a snow-covered mound. She kicked away a bit of snow to see what it was, and under the snow was the frozen body of Topsie. In a drunken stupor, she had wandered out of her house without a parka. Unable to find her way, she had frozen to death twenty feet from shelter. Topsie was no more than nineteen years old.

Bessie's husband smashed in her head during a drunken fight, and she was brought to the nursing station where she died without making a statement. Bessie's husband came to me sobbing. Would I arrange the funeral? At the service he sat in the front row weeping. Afterwards, often when he was intoxicated he'd jump on his Honda and go up to the burial site to weep over Bessie's grave.

Jimmy was an Eskimo man who had returned to the village after serving a jail sentence on a murder charge. He had come back to rehabilitate himself, with the hope of again taking his place in community life. But soon he was trapped in the drinking scene. The drinking worsened in Jimmy's life with both he and Mary, the woman he lived with, often involved in drunken parties.

One night, in a state of drunkenness, he was angry with her and took her out on the ice to beat her up. Somehow his snowmobile crashed into a standing truck, temporarily knocking Jimmy out. But Mary scrambled off the snowmobile and ran to my home. About two o'clock in the morning she stumbled in the kitchen door, covered with blood and obviously intoxicated. I already had an Eskimo woman and her four children staying with me that night because her husband was drunk and fighting and they had run away from him for the night. So what was one more? We soon put Mary to bed.

I thought the next morning she would want to hurry back to Jimmy. But Mary had a desperate story to tell. "When he is drunk he will kill me!" From instances of violence in the past, I knew she spoke the truth.

"Will you please help me, Kayy?" she pled. "Help me get away from this village. There is nowhere I can go, no one will help me in this town." I knew this was true, for everyone feared Jimmy because of his past history. When desperate humanity is on your doorstep, can you say, "Go away!" and then later regret it at the funeral? I promised Mary I would help her leave the village.

A government employee arranged for a ticket to be purchased for the trip to Tuk where Mary's relatives were among the Christian families. They met her and looked after her, and later on she met a Christian man who was to become her husband.

A few nights later, a strange thing happened. About midnight my door again burst open and another bloody face met me. This time it was Jimmy's! He was intoxicated, bleeding and crying.

I looked after his cuts, then sat down to drink coffee with him. Jimmy poured his heart out to me weeping, as he told me of his troubles and struggles in life, how he seemed to be unable to break out of this tragic situation.

With as many as ten deaths a year in the area directly attributable to drunkenness, one evening a public meeting was called to discuss the alcohol problem. This was debated at length and then the question was asked, "Does anyone have a solution to suggest?" Dead silence.

Finally Ron Duffy stood up. "I know how I handled the alcohol problem. I went to the Pentecostal church and got saved. That was the end of my alcohol problem." One after another, the Eskimos jumped to their feet, testifying to how they had been saved and delivered. "Boy, this sure is the best meeting I've been in," one council member enthused.

Later some of the whites were furious with me. "You sure engineered that meeting nicely," they accused. Actually I hadn't done a thing. True, I had canceled the prayer service because I felt we should all be at that community meeting. But I certainly had not prompted the Eskimos on what role they should play.

Only one Eskimo spoke out in favor of liquor. "What harm is there? It's fun to go out and get drunk," he insisted. Not long after, this "fun-loving" Eskimo committed suicide.

CHAPTER 25

Youth Work and
Community Involvement

With so many home problems, with the children not in school and out on the streets all hours of the night and day, we decided we needed a more active summer program for our young people. The idea of a camp fascinated them and there was no trouble finding the thirty children, ages ten to eighteen, that we decided to have in our first group. Finding adequate camping equipment was not as easy. We finally sewed two tents together to make one larger twelve-by-twenty-eight-foot tent that served as cookhouse, dining room, chapel and recreation hall. The other equipment was mostly makeshift.

In August when the ice was finally out of the bay, we loaded the children and our supplies into canoes and speedboats of all shapes and sizes for the six-mile trip across the open inlet to our campsite. I sat in the canoe and watched the waves rising, and prayed. We'd chosen a flat-topped rise where there was space to put up the big tent plus several sleeping tents, the boys on one side of the big top, the girls on the other.

With the high winds at Cambridge Bay, it was quite a challenge to keep those tents from blowing into the ocean. That year, Marian and I served as camp cooks, counselors, and sports directors for this arctic summer olympics including volleyball and baseball games, and 100-yard dashes. We were swimming instructors too. The children insisted on going in the Arctic Ocean every day in spite of icy winds with air temperatures ranging from 50 to 60 degrees. The ocean temperature? C-O-L-D. Perhaps 45 degrees.

Camping in the Arctic can be very simple. Caribou skins are laid on the rough, stony ground, with sleeping bags rolled out on top, the parkas scrunched up for pillows. The boys and girls sleep in their underwear and share soap and towels.

We brought out two primus stoves to cook on, three burners in all, and the meals were simple, yet everyone enjoyed them immensely. There was always rolled oats for breakfast, for the other meals macaroni, stews, or their favorite pork and beans with canned weiners. Sometimes we had boiled fish with instant potatoes and peas, and always bannock, tea and jam.

There were no tables to set. We brought bowls and spoons from the chapel and the youngsters dragged in large stones and sundry boxes to sit on. It was a crowded situation, but Eskimo children are experts in tent life and never spill a thing.

Morning wake-up was about nine-thirty, or whenever the campers began to stir. We let them sleep in because where they live, their days don't terminate until midnight at the earliest with the sun still high in the sky. After a wash-up in the ocean we had breakfast, followed by camp clean-up. This was fairly simple. There were dishes, but no toilets to clean. The boys went over the hill one way, the girls the other. They loved tent inspection, and the group with the highest points got a special award at the end of camp—a bag of candy each and perhaps a Bible plaque.

Then we would gather in the big tent for song time and Bible classes. How they loved the action choruses—''I don't want to be a Jonah and be swallowed by a whale,'' and ''There's a fountain flowing deep and wide.'' And then we would have Scripture memorization—it was astounding how they could memorize. A surprising number would spend their free time at this.

The rest of the day was devoted to games, sports and crafts. We did the plaques with spray-painted alphabet macaroni, and varnished Popsicle stick pencil holders.

After supper came the high point of the camp program—the campfire itself. But when you are hundreds of miles north of the tree line, what do you do for wood? Before camp, we had scrounged all over Cambridge Bay for every possible scrap, and then carried it out to camp with us. There would be no real dark till much later in the year.

So with the sun beaming brightly we'd stand huddled around the fire (it was too cold to sit). One of the boys would play the guitar and the young people would lustily clap and sing along. The fire wouldn't last too long, but before the embers died away, we'd roast marshmallows or weiners speared on pieces of wood from apple crates.

The night was still young (by Eskimo standards), so again we'd gather in the big tent, spreading caribou skins for the children to sit on. We would sing some more because the Eskimos never tire of singing. Then they would listen intently to a brief gospel message.

As the sun would still be shining, we had to invent more activities, perhaps a treasure hunt with clues tucked under the stones leading over the hills and around the lake. The prize? A bag of peanuts or toffee. With good planning, that would keep them going for forty-five minutes. Sometimes there'd be a ball game, with their own tundra rules, and this could go on till midnight. When the whistle blew, everyone knew it was hot chocolate time, then time to hit the sack—or in their case, the caribou skins.

It was an exhausting program for the leaders, but rewarding when we saw the many children receiving spiritually from the Lord as well as enjoying good clean fun.

The missionary's role in the Arctic is not a spiritual one, but overlaps into many areas of community life. In 1968 I was given the opportunity to serve as chairman of Cambridge Bay's northwest centennial celebrations. This committee of Eskimos and whites decided that for our special centennial project we would purchase much needed playground equipment for the children. We would do this by hosting an arctic feast, featuring all kinds of Eskimo delicacies, cooked and raw, prepared by the Eskimo people.

Together we planned several other activities—a snowmobile race banquet, a luncheon for Prime Minister Trudeau—and, at the end of the year, we were able to produce enough money to buy the playground equipment as a lasting memorial for the centennial celebration. The Eskimo children totally enjoy their new merry-go-rounds, swings, teeter-totters and, especially, their slide.

In my early years in Cambridge Bay I had introduced Girl Guides and Brownies. Meeting after school, the government administrator's wife was "Brown Owl for the Brownies" and I took charge of the Guides. Later we were able to train Eskimo women to help in the leadership roles. At the first enrollment how thrilled the children were to be in uniform and it was a most festive evening for the girls and their parents.

I recall another time when several Eskimo parents came to me about a problem in the school. These were not only people from our own church, but also some Catholic and Anglican families as well. They were disturbed that the new school principal had opened a smoking room for seventh and eighth graders. The Eskimos felt strongly about this; they had sent their children to learn to read and write, but they had not sent them to school to learn how to smoke.

The local Anglican minister and I went to the principal to discuss this problem, but the principal could not see that this was a problem. For him it was a "step of development and an opportunity to teach responsibility to the children."

The Eskimo parents continued to voice their opinion against this to me. They didn't feel they knew the principal well enough to go to him themselves. They became very concerned, so we called a meeting of all the parents who had children in those grades. Ninety-five percent of them turned out.

We discussed the problem and all agreed that something should be done. My main concern was to turn this situation into a learning experience for the people, showing them how they could deal with any situation they felt was unjust for themselves or their families. I explained that when talking does not produce action, then we should work with pen and paper, and I showed them how to draw up a petition that they could sign and take to the school principal.

They readily responded to the petition idea. In no time we had it written in English and then translated as accurately as possible into Eskimo. It was carefully read to them so they could fully understand it. Then I simply laid the petition on the table and said, "Now, if any want to sign this, you can; if you don't want to sign it and commit yourself, you don't have to. It's up to you." As I left the room I could hear a buzz of excited conversation. One by one every parent in the room signed.

Later I felt we needed the backing of all the other parents in the school, because the younger children also were observing this smoking room in action. Ninety-seven percent of all parents were in agreement with the petition.

Another meeting of the children's parents was called and again they were very verbal about their feelings. Soon the smoking room was turned into a science lab.

My life often took on many interesting twists. Sometimes the members of the Eskimo council would come and ask for guidance when they felt they were being outmaneuvered by private enterprise. They often felt these men were trying to hold onto, or take over, jobs that an Eskimo man was capable of doing. Sometimes this entailed giving them tips and a basic understanding of parliamentary procedure, assisting them in framing the right motions, and teaching them to run their own affairs, and thereby control their own destiny.

This was always paramount: helping the Eskimo and teaching him how to assist his own people. It has been interesting to note the many Christian Eskimos who have been promoted to positions of prominence in various organizations as they give leadership to their own people.

In the last decades, Eskimo womanhood has been changed also, with women no longer staying in the background. Rather, many of them are assuming leadership roles with the men in arctic living. Some are in government positions, many are on settlement councils and in many instances, the Christian women have the strongest voices to be heard.

Ruth, along with being a housemother, has also served on the education advisory board, deciding on policy affecting the school. Doris's contribution on the settlement council has already been mentioned. Louisa, too, is a fine example. She had come to Cambridge Bay from Perry Island and spoke very little English. After a few years she became a Christian and obtained a good government job in charge of the transient center. Her knowledge of English improved, along with her confidence. She became a more outgoing person and was elected to the settlement council where she spoke out strongly and fearlessly on issues that concern the Inuit. In 1968, a very colorful couple moved to Cambridge Bay. Sammy and Doris Angohiatok had been working for some time on the DEW line. Doris was a highly intelligent Eskimo woman with a lot going for her. She was fluent in both English and Eskimo. Her husband, Sammy, had a very different background. Born and raised in an igloo, he had never had the opportunity of attending school. He was indeed a man of the land who lived in the traditional style of the Eskimos, trapping and hunting.

One day Sammy discovered the DEW line and was fascinated to learn that Eskimos were being taught to operate heavy-duty equipment and to do other maintenance work. Soon he and Doris moved to a DEW line site and Sammy quickly learned the art of maneuvering the snow movers, big Cats and dump trucks.

But Sammy and Doris acquired something else that they had never had before—the white man's liquor. At first it was just a little social drink once in a while, but soon they were involved in more and more parties. The drinking increased until it reached the stage, Doris later told me, that in the morning instead of reaching for a cup of coffee or tea, she reached for a can of beer. It became common for their children to see their parents passed out on the floor after drinking all night.

Finally Sammy left his job and they moved to Cambridge Bay. Here it was the same story—going from party to party, always looking for another drink or perhaps another poker game. These vices were eating away the very life and happiness of this fine, young couple.

One evening both Sammy and Doris attended our service. Like many of the Eskimos, Doris thought Kayy Gordon was a man, and decided to come and hear what "he" had to say. Naturally, she was shocked to discover that I was a woman preacher. And she was even more surprised by the form of worship in our church. Never had she heard such happy singing and joyful testimonies.

One Wednesday afternoon in the spring, she and Sammy were out hunting ptarmigan, an arctic bird about the size of a partridge. In the late afternoon she said, "Sammy, let's go home early. I want to go to church tonight."

We had already begun the singing and it was almost time for John Maksagak to bring the message when the chapel door burst open and in came Doris. She was still in her travel clothes. Obviously, she very much wanted to be in that service.

The message was hardly over and the altar call just given when Doris arose from her seat and purposefully walked to the altar to surrender her life to Jesus Christ. It was Doris's decision day. After a few minutes of prayer she arose from the altar a new creature in Christ.

Old things immediately began to pass away. Doris lost her desire for drink. She had been an avid gambler, but that night she sat through a poker game in her own home with no desire to participate. Jesus had changed her life. It was obvious to the whole community that something had happened to Doris, for she was an extrovert, always the life of any party. Now she was talking about a new-found faith in Jesus.

Doris believed God for her whole household, praying first for her husband, and after several months Sammy, too, was saved.

What a transformation in that home! Now the two of them were serving the Lord together. Because of the extreme drinking problem before they were saved, there never seemed to be enough money to buy new clothes for the kids or to put food on the table. But now all this was changing. The teenage boys came home from the Inuvik hostel where they attended school, and were amazed at their parents. "Oh, mom and dad," they exclaimed, "it's so great to see you like this. Don't ever give up!"

Doris became a very strong witness for Christ. No matter who was in her home, whether an Eskimo or a white person, she was able to bring out a very natural witness for the Lord. Their little house was truly a lighthouse, and many people in difficulty or when searching for God would visit the Angohiatok home.

One day Doris and Sammy had gone out to hunt caribou because their food supply was low. Their snowmobile was old and giving them trouble so they couldn't keep up with the other hunters. Suddenly the engine failed, then died. Because Sammy had been out of work for some time, he didn't have a good supply of parts to take along with him. In fact, he had next to nothing.

So here they were, fifty miles out on the barrens alone with little food. It was bitterly cold with a strong wind blowing. Doris was not in a very good physical condition. Following tuberculosis, she had had extensive surgery. One lung was collapsed and the other was only partially functioning. There was no way she could make the fifty-mile hike home to Cambridge Bay.

Sammy pitched his tent and checked over the snowmobile once more. There was nothing he could do to repair it. He also noted that the other hunters had taken off in different directions and would not be expected to pass by Sammy's tent now.

Instead of becoming frustrated or desperate, Sammy told Doris he was going to lie down and sleep for a while. With that, he pulled off the caribou skins that were lashed on the sled and laid them on the snow platform in the tent. Covering himself with a little blanket, he curled up and went to sleep. But first he prayed and asked the Lord to make a way in this impossible wilderness.

Soon Sammy fell into a deep sleep, and as he slept he had a dream. In his dream he saw a man in white walking toward him and then over to the snowmobile. The man in white began giving instructions and showed Sammy how he could repair the broken piece without a soldering iron. Then he showed Sammy how to fix the other damaged area. Sammy watched and listened intently. Suddenly the "man in white" disappeared.

With that Sammy awakened. Quickly he jumped up and rushed outside to his vehicle. Step by step he went through the intricate, unusual procedures outlined by the heavenly visitor in his dream. So confident was Sammy that the snowmobile would run again that he started to sing and praise the Lord in his native tongue as he worked.

In addition to the broken pulley arm, the belt on the engine was gone, but the "man in white" had told Sammy that a quarter inch belt would work instead of the usual one-and-a-half inch belt. He pulled the starting rope, the motor turned over and began to run like a charm.

Quickly Sammy and Doris packed up their belongings, dismantled the tent and lashed it onto the sled. But before leaving they knelt in the snow and thanked God for His goodness and mercy. With hearts full of faith and confidence, they started for home, never once doubting that it would all hold together on the trip over the rough terrain.

Back at the village, a mechanic examined the snowmobile and shook his head. "It's incredible!" he cried out. That evening there was no small time of rejoicing in the little chapel as Sammy told of God's miraculous provision in his hour of dire need.

But there were still other members of Doris's family who were not saved. Her mother, Akana, was next on the list. Doris prayed intently for her mother and she, too, finally came to Christ. A short time later, Akana had to go to a hospital in Edmonton for T.B. treatment. Often our ways are not God's ways. During those long days and weeks in the hospital, Akana deepened in her Christian faith. She returned home a strong, radiant Christian ready to witness to her people.

Nor would the family be satisfied to have just the mother saved. Before the year was out, Doris's brother, Simon, was saved along with the teenage boys and their younger brother, Gary. Thus, a whole household was transformed by the power of God.

Only one remained unsaved and that was Hogaluk, Doris's father. Hogaluk had other ideas: "I was born an Anglican, I've lived an Anglican and I'll die an Anglican," was his affirmation. But Doris prayed on, Akana prayed on, Sammy prayed on. They all believed that God would save Hogaluk.

A year passed by and Hogaluk seemed the same, a very friendly man, a very witty man, but not ready to commit his life to God. One day he became sick and the doctor diagnosed his illness as cancer. It was a terrible blow to the family. Their father had cancer! Doris prayed harder than ever: "God, please don't let my dad die until he has a real experience with you."

The Holy Spirit was working on Hogaluk's heart. Alone in his little bedroom during the early hours of one morning, suffering intense pain, with cancer racking his body, Hogaluk prayed: "Oh, God, if it's really true, let the Lord make himself known to me and I will serve Him." That very night, somehow, God made himself real to old Hogaluk, and there in the quietness of his sickroom he met the living God in a personal way.

The next day Doris sent for me. I expected the worst, but found a tremendous change had taken place in Hogaluk. As I entered his sickroom I sensed a holy hush within. Heaven filled that place. The cancer had reduced Hogaluk to mere skin and bones, but he was sitting up in bed, his face fairly shining as he told how two angels had visited him and told him: "Hogaluk, you must be a Christian not just from the outside, but from deep within." He responded and found the peace and joy of God. Instantly, the pain left his body.

The next few days of his life, his last, were spent witnessing to every person who came into his house. According to Eskimo custom, when someone is about to die, the family and many friends come in for a final visit. As they streamed in and out of Hogaluk's room, it seemed that a new strength from above was given him. He hardly ate or slept for days, but just poured out his heart to his people. Young and old, Hogaluk told them of his experience with God, admonishing everyone to serve the Lord. His only regret in life was that he had wasted so many years. The presence of God was so real in that little room that no one wanted to leave. It was a beautiful experience.

A few days later Hogaluk told Doris, "I think I'm going to leave you tomorrow, but don't be sad. Don't cry for me, for last night the Lord let me see a beautiful place where everything is clean and spotless and pure. He told me He's going to take me there." About four o'clock in the morning my phone rang. Hogaluk had fallen asleep, passing into the presence of the Lord. God had answered the continuing prayers of Doris and Sammy, and had reached out His hand and saved their whole household for God.

In time, the leaders of the community realized the potential in Doris and approached her to consider becoming legal interpreter in Ottawa. She declined this job but was then elected by the people to serve on the community council. She also served on the centennial committee and the housing committee of which John Maksagak was chairman. Because she speaks up clearly and forcibly on many issues, Doris often is chosen to represent her people at government meetings in Yellowknife. She has become a strong voice and in many ways is making a worthwhile contribution to the general welfare of the Inuit in Cambridge Bay.

When the gospel transforms Eskimo lives, a stability and a strength is given them from above. Soon this is recognized by others. As one government official put it, "If you want a steady worker, hire a Pentecostal." Or as an R.C.M.P. constable wryly remarked when he overheard the Pentecostals being criticized, "Say what you like. These people don't appear on my trouble lists."

CHAPTER 26

Powers of the Anagkok

Much of arctic culture is very private to the Eskimo and is not readily divulged to, or understood by, outsiders. One of these private matters is the world of spirits.

Their myths, legends and folklore are all built around the supernatural forces that have dominated their world. In each community there has been at least one person possessing special powers of *anagkok*—intuitive powers that could curse. Areas of mystery and fear lurk just below the surface.

One day a group of Eskimo girls and I were out on the ice and were going to climb Mount Pelly. As we approached, they exclaimed, "*Irigi*! *Irigi*! (scary). To climb the mountain we are afraid."

Then they told me the legend of the mountain, that originally Mount Pelly was a male giant and there was a smaller hill nearby called Lady Pelly, a female giant. They walked about for a long time, then settled into mountains, so the mountain has a special spirit that was to be feared.

Over in the western Arctic at Tuk an old woman, Ely Dick, was a recognized *anagkok*. Her special power was to frighten people by making them see polar bears. Helen Magsagak shared a room with Ely Dick in the hospital at Aklavik, and suddenly, coming out from under a bed in the ward, Helen saw an angry polar bear.

Immediately, Helen cried out, "Ely Dick, I'm a Christian now, so you'd better stop using *anagkok*. You can't scare me because I have a greater power."

The polar bear evaporated. Ely Dick apologized to Helen, turned over and went to sleep.

Silas Kanegana, one of the reindeer herders, had a very strong faith in God following his conversion. Almost immediately after his conversion Silas renounced his belief in the power of the *anagkok*.

A short time later, while herding reindeer in the Mackenzie Delta, Silas was camped next to the tent of an old man, Morris. He had special powers as an *anagkok* to make people violently sick to their stomachs.

One day Silas confronted him: "Your *anagkok* powers are useless. The power of Jesus Christ is far greater." Morris was very angry and went back into his tent and proceeded to put a curse on Silas. But a strange thing happened. Instead of Silas getting sick, the old man himself became violently ill and called Silas in. "Will you pray for me, Silas? The power of your Jesus Christ is too strong for my *anagkok* powers!" Silas prayed. Almost instantly the severe stomach pains left Morris and he recovered.

During my first year at Cambridge Bay, I went out to visit a primitive Eskimo group at their spring fish camp. A few had been converted in Cambridge Bay, but the local *anagkok*, an old woman (and it is remarkable how many of those having these special powers are women) was rather hostile to me.

I was camping with a family who recently had begun to serve the Lord. One night I was awakened by the clanging and banging of pots and cans outside my tent. I could hear this old Eskimo woman's voice chanting and I assumed she was endeavoring to put a curse on me. I felt nothing, but remained quiet in my sleeping bag, praying. The incident passed and I didn't arise until my normal time. Prior to leaving, I made a special point to go into the old woman's tent and talked with her about the power of Jesus Christ. I shared her ptarmigan soup and left the camp with no ill effects.

In Cambridge Bay, one man was said to have the special *anagkok* power of flying. No one had seen him fly, of course, but they feared that he could fly and so he could be with them anywhere at any moment. This made the Eskimos fear him. Some white fox pelts had been stolen from the Hudson's Bay, the first theft the company had ever had in Cambridge Bay, and the mounted police had pursued every angle unsuccessfully.

Finally, in desperation, one of the constables turned to this local *anagkok* for help. He was very happy to lend his services, for remuneration, confident he could locate the thief. After all, he had power to fly, hadn't he? He led the police to a house and they tore up the floor, but found no pelts. They followed a suspect on his trapline, but this too was a dead end. Finally the case was abandoned as unsolvable.

When a famous hunter or highly respected person in the community dies, the next child born usually bears the name of that esteemed person. The Eskimos believe the spirit of the deceased person will enter into the child so they, too, will become mighty. In some instances this definitely influences the way the Eskimo child is treated. In Tuk I recall seeing an Eskimo man tenderly refer to his child as "my mother" and he would refer to her in the same way as to his respected mother.

In Christian circles, because the Eskimo people are very warm and sentimental, we do not repudiate this practice of naming children after departed loved ones. But we do teach them that after death, the spirit returns to God, and each child has his own spirit.

This realm of the spirits is one that even the Christian Eskimos are reluctant to talk about. It's a very private area of their lives, with deeply entrenched fears that even the strong Christians have to battle with from time to time.

We were having our usual fellowship after the Sunday evening service one cold December night when the door burst open and Susie stumbled in babbling hysterically, "*Amamega tokoyok . . . my mother is dead!*" Susie had returned to her eight-by-eight-foot shack to find her mother, Aitoak, sprawled face down on the floor, unmoving, semi-frozen. Susie had run back to my house with the news.

I called the doctor who stopped by to pick me up in the bombardier. The houseful of Eskimos decided they too should go down to Susie's house, so all fifteen piled into the bombardier and we set off. Among them was Doris, my interpreter. We arrived at the tiny, unlighted, unheated shack, with everyone pushing in till there was no room for the doctor. I asked them to please wait in the little porch while I held the flashlight for the doctor.

As he turned the body over for examination, we could see the ruff around her parka was soaked in congealing blood. The jugular vein had been cut, and in Aitoak's hand we saw a knife. Suicide! I heard a gasp from the porch, and suddenly they all took off, fleeing in terror. I stepped out to call Doris to help interpret. She was nowhere in sight. The fright of suicide had sent her to her house and there was no way I could persuade her to leave it that night.

Several of the people told me they felt a strange sense of foreboding and fear that prevented them from sleeping. The young Eskimo boy staying with us asked, "Couldn't we please sleep with the lights on?" The Eskimos seemed to sense a sinister presence that night.

It was difficult to get anyone to help move the body, whereas ordinarily they all would freely offer their services and want to be a part of burial arrangements. Only the immediate family and a handful of Christians attended the funeral instead of the usual large attendance.

Months later the Eskimos told me why they felt Aitoak had taken her life. It seems that she had been out on the DEW line visiting with an Eskimo family who worked there and she had been involved in some misdemeanor. One of the whites had warned, probably jokingly, "Aitoak, you'd better be careful or you'll be sent south."

Aitoak was old and illiterate, and this fear of being sent south preyed on her mind. Like all Eskimos, she wanted to die among her own people. So she took her knife and slit her throat.

Today, especially in the western Arctic, the power of the *anagkok* has been almost broken. Even in the more superstitious eastern Arctic this *anagkok* power is definitely receding because of the swelling tide of the strong moving of God in the midst of the Eskimos.

Early in my days in the Arctic, a young girl rushed in. "My mother is dying," she said. "She can't breathe good. Please come quick."

Immediately I asked, "Did you call the nurse?"

"It is not that kind of sickness," she replied.

I ran to John's house because I would need an interpreter, and together we trudged for ten minutes through the snow to the far side of the village. There was an unnatural silence about the little shack, and as we stepped inside, we both felt an eerie, oppressive presence. The dimly-lit shack was already crowded with relatives and neighbors sitting around in uneasy silence, gravely concerned. The woman, Lucy, seemed unaware of our presence as she sat on a chair wearing her parka and mitts, staring straight ahead. She was in a trance, her breathing very labored and uneven, stopping at times.

The tension mounted as we laid our hands on her. Suddenly John began to pray authoritatively in Eskimo. "In the name of Jesus, evil spirit, *come out of her!*" he commanded.

Lucy shook herself, took a deep breath, and looked around startled, as if waking from a long sleep. The trance had been broken. Lucy had been set free by the power of God.

And to the Uttermost

CHAPTER 27

Bible School

One day in January, 1972, Florence Erickson, a Bible teacher visiting from the south, looked out the window and exclaimed, "Kayy, look at the beautiful red glow in the sky!" It meant that the long winter night was soon to be broken by the rise of the sun returning to the north. Somehow as I gazed across the darkened, snow-covered landscape and saw that red glow, something within me witnessed that there would be a new light shining in the Arctic. A new spiritual light would extend across the barren lands and reach out to many Eskimo people.

The work in Cambridge Bay was being abundantly blessed of God with approximately 100 attending Sunday services regularly. Yet always before me was the unfinished task of reaching the unreached, the 70 percent of our Eskimos who had not yet heard a clear presentation of the simple gospel message.

But to do this we had to begin training Eskimo Christians to take the message to their own people. We missionaries could not do the job, and even if we could, we couldn't do it half as well as the natives. Somehow we had to get going on our long-dreamed-of Bible school.

Finally, it seemed that the opportune moment had come. Many young people, including couples, were very anxious to learn God's ways and God's Word. We had moved into the spacious apartment above the church, so the old house could make an ideal classroom.

A fine in-depth Bible teacher, Florence Erickson, had come in to help me. In Taiwan, Florence had been mightily used of God as she ministered on the baptism in the Holy Ghost, with many Taiwanese receiving this infilling of the Spirit. Many of our Eskimos who were faithfully serving the Lord had not yet received this blessing so before we began the Bible school, Florence held special meetings showing our people how they, too, could experience this anointing from God.

As Florence ministered and then as we prayed with the Eskimo people, God began to do a miraculous work. First it was one or two at the altar being wonderfully baptized with the Holy Ghost. Then in the prayer meetings that followed, many more were filled to overflowing with this experience from God. It was moving so quickly and so supernaturally that we both knew it had to be the hand of the Lord. The Eskimos would literally be overcome by God's power, some falling forward on the altar as they overflowed with the presence of God.

Others would be beside themselves with joy, as in Bible times. On the day of Pentecost, some mocked this outpouring, saying, "They're drunk, that's all!" But Peter replied, "No! What you see this morning was predicted centuries ago by the prophet Joel—'In the last days,' God said, 'I will pour out my Holy Spirit upon all mankind, and your sons and daughters shall prophesy, and your young men shall see visions, and your old men dream dreams' " (Acts 2:13, 16-17 TLB).

Like the disciples of old, God's servants in the Arctic were being "filled with joy and with the Holy Spirit" (Acts 13:52 TLB).

One night, three or four were receiving the baptism in the Holy

Ghost, praising God and speaking in other tongues. One of them was Sammy, Doris's husband. A little later on, her oldest teenage boy received this anointing. This was too much for Doris, for she herself had not yet been so blessed. She went out of the church very disturbed. "I'll never go near that church again," she decided. "God always denies me this blessing."

As she was trekking home over the snow and the frozen lake, Doris reached into her pocket for a cigarette (she had not yet been able to get rid of the smoking habit), and as she reached for this cigarette, Doris felt as if the Lord spoke to her and said, "What do you want, cigarettes or the Holy Ghost?"

"I want the Holy Ghost!" Doris cried out, and with that she took her pack of cigarettes and flung it in the snowdrift, turned on her heel and came rushing back into the church.

It was now about eleven o'clock and we were ready to leave when Doris burst in. "Don't stop praying. Pray for me." In answer to prayer that night, Doris was completely delivered from her smoking.

The next night she was back again for our prayer meeting. How she thanked the Lord from the depths of her heart for all He had done for her! As she was worshiping God and praying for others, the presence of the Lord enfolded her and she received a wonderful baptism in the Holy Ghost. She was so full of this experience that she was bubbling over, speaking in other tongues, worshiping God. As she went home it continued, and apparently they had a prayer meeting most of the night when as a household they rejoiced and prayed together in their new-found experience in God. A new strength came into Doris. An even clearer and sharper witness was born in her heart; her boldness was intensified and the joy of the Lord radiated from her life.

The next day she was still overjoyed. The telephone rang and in her zeal Doris answered, "Praise the Lord!" There was a stunned silence at the other end and finally a very British voice replied, "Indeed, the Lord's name is to be praised!" It was the local administrator calling Doris about a conference, but she was just rejoicing in God's goodness.

Another beautiful sight at the altar came as Gwen and George were seeking God for the baptism in the Holy Ghost. George was kneeling on one side of the altar and Gwen on the other. Just a few years previously these two young people had been wonderfully saved, their desires changed, their lives transformed.

Two years earlier I had married them, the first wedding in the new church. It had been a beautiful Christian wedding, and now they were both asking God to grant them a further experience. Unknown to each other, at opposite ends of the altar, almost simultaneously they both received the Holy Ghost and began to speak in tongues at the same time. Without question, they were the happiest couple in Cambridge Bay that night.

That same winter, George and Gwen were to face a crisis in their lives. As a teenager, Gwen had become very verbal in her anti-Christian views. Then through the death of her little niece, Gwen began coming to church and very shortly afterwards had become a Christian along with the other members of her family. She was a very solid one, purposefully setting herself to serve God.

Although she was young, Gwen was highly intelligent and very mature, and at sixteen she and George were married. Together they set up a Christian home and the next year they were blessed with a baby daughter, Georgina. Gwen and George treated this baby like a little princess.

When little Georgina was a year old she became very ill with a respiratory problem and was rushed to the nursing station. George called me. He couldn't leave his job, but would I join Gwen?

We simply prayed that God's hand would be on that child and spare the little life according to His will. We felt the witness in our hearts that God had granted our request.

Unknown to us, as we were praying, the baby had taken a turn for the worse. The records state that she actually stopped breathing and was feared dead. But suddenly little Georgina began breathing and today she is a normal child.

John Maksagak's oldest boy, Harry, had now grown up and taken a beautiful wife, Mary Rose, an Indian princess from Yellowknife. She had followed Harry to Eskimo land and like Ruth of old, his people became her people. Mary Rose had heard the gospel for the first time in Cambridge Bay.

One night as her father-in-law was preaching, Mary Rose saw tears in his eyes. With great love and tenderness, John Maksagak spoke to the people of their need of Jesus Christ. This greatly impressed Mary Rose. She had been reared as a staunch Catholic, but she couldn't remember a priest being so moved when he presented a message. Never had she seen any minister so stirred as he talked about God. This struck a note in Mary Rose's heart. She listened intently and at the end of the service, as the Holy Spirit convicted her of her need of Christ, she made her way to the altar and publicly confessed Christ. A tremendous change came in her life.

By the time the move of the Holy Ghost was at its peak in Cambridge Bay, Mary Rose was four or five months pregnant with her first child. She had been quite sick and was weak in her body. It was a tender sight to see her at the altar praying to God for this wonderful experience. Her strong, young husband had his arms around her, holding her, praying for her. And then in a beautiful and gentle way, the Holy Spirit visited Mary Rose and granted her heart's desire. She was wonderfully baptized with the Holy Ghost and a lovely melodious tongue flowed from her as she received bountifully from God. This young woman's life was strengthened, and in the days that followed, no matter how strong the winds of adversity blew, she stood true to God, looking forward to the day when she could share Christ with her own Indian people.

Not only did the moving of the Holy Spirit affect the adult population, but the teenage Eskimos received their portion from the Lord too. It was a stirring sight to see these teenage girls and fellows gather, earnestly seeking God to fill their lives with power and strength that would keep them in the times of temptation and testing that might lie ahead. Many of them were wonderfully filled with the Holy Ghost around those altars and in the prayer room. God visited them and seemed to grant them a special anointing of joy. The joy of the Lord became their strength (Neh. 8:10).

I recall one night after a meeting, fifteen or twenty of these teenagers left the church singing gospel songs, making the streets of the little village ring with choruses of joy. "It's the Holy Ghost and fire, and it's keeping me alive, Jesus is keeping me alive!"

They went from house to house, witnessing to their own people of the new strengthening power that the Holy Spirit had brought into their lives. As a result many people came to the church services. It was standing room only night after night.

These teenagers were a tremendous influence in this Eskimo village. Their lives had been transformed with a radiant joy that attracted others.

Within these teenagers was born a great desire to win others for Christ. "Can we have our own prayer meeting?" they asked. What an inspiration and challenge it was to hear those young people crying to God from the depths of their being for other teenagers, for their unsaved parents, their loved ones. Some were from the outlying camps, and they prayed that God would visit every camp, moving in every home. Many people were saved as a result. The altars were lined night after night with hungry Eskimos reaching out to the Lord. Children would sometimes be kneeling beside their grandparents. The old and young together, hungry for more from God, were seeking God's presence.

For about a month this special outpouring of God's Spirit came upon the people and it was in this atmosphere that we began the Bible school program.

The overflow of God's anointing and presence was very evident in every session as we studied God's Word. We saw the Scripture literally come to pass: "The Holy Ghost, whom the Father will send in my name, he shall teach you all things, and bring all things to your remembrance, whatsoever I have said unto you" (John 14:26 KJV).

Those people were not only taught by earthly teachers; their understanding was illuminated by the Holy Ghost. They were able to grasp in-depth teaching much more quickly than we had seen in the south. Florence and I were both amazed.

We planned a three-year certificate program, made up of three-hour sessions, two evenings each week for the six winter months. An overall coverage of the Old and New Testaments was our aim. We desired to teach our students the basic doctrines of salvation, healing, the Holy Spirit, praise, and soul winning.

Marian taught on the life of Christ; I taught subjects relating to the end-time—the return of Christ and fulfilled prophecy. We introduced Bible marking so they could identify different subjects in their Bibles more quickly. There were courses covering Scripture memorization, how to lead a Bible study, homiletics, song leading, and youth leadership. To give the students a well-rounded perspective of God's Word, each term we brought in a guest teacher from the south. The evenings seemed to pass too quickly as God's Spirit illuminated His Word afresh.

During the first spring of Bible school I planned to take one of our students, Doris, with me to answer a call from another village, Holman Island, on the northwest coast of Victoria Island. We did not know what to expect as no one knew of our coming. I explained to Doris that we would go into the village and make acquaintances from house to house, looking to the Lord to make our witnessing fruitful eventually. I was concerned that our students not imagine that they could go out and suddenly turn the north upside down, that everything would happen immediately.

Eskimo custom is to visit the old people first when arriving in a village. Doris and I set out to do this, and found that one old lady, Kalvak, was very sick. Kalvak is an artist of international fame, with her name appearing on Eskimo prints in galleries around the world. Doris explained to her that our only power was in God, that only God could make her well. And then at Kalvak's request we prayed for her. The next day we saw her daughter and asked how Kalvak was.

"Worse," her daughter replied glumly. This was quite a blow to Doris. After all, this was her first missionary endeavor and she hadn't quite anticipated this. I said to her, "Just wait. Things can turn." A little later Kalvak herself called us and explained that she was feeling so much better. This was a good sign, a meaningful sign to the Eskimo people, that we did have something to offer.

As we went from door to door, I was amazed at Doris's ability to witness so beautifully and inoffensively, yet effectively, to her own people. Before I could put my landing gear down as it were, and get seated in the home, Doris had already very naturally opened a conversation about the things of God with the people. Not only did they respond to our visits as we covered every house in that village, but also we were invited to have our house meetings in a different home each night. This was beyond our expectations.

What a joy it was to gather in their homes for these house meetings, usually packed with Eskimos, with many children crowding in the bedroom behind us. When Doris stood to lead the singing she couldn't move an inch, nor could I when I stood up to preach.

Outside, many Eskimos crowded in close to the window, straining to hear the singing, to catch a sound of the gospel. It was 40 below but they stood there for forty-five minutes. This is spiritual hunger. This is true desire for God. It was a sight I shall never forget.

After the service one old man said to me, "We have heard much teaching on religion, but I've never heard it as simple as it was tonight. We have never heard this message before."

At the end of five nights of house meetings, we couldn't leave the community without giving an opportunity for the people to make a public stand for Christ. I really didn't expect to see many respond; I thought maybe one or two who had been especially interested would.

As simply as possible I asked, "Are you really ready to meet God? Do you know for certain your sins are forgiven? Tonight Jesus is waiting to help you. How many would like to be saved tonight? If so, turn around and kneel for prayer where you are," I said to them. To my astonishment at least twenty people responded, singing in Eskimo, "*Kaiyunga* Jesus, *Kaiyunga Ilingnon* . . . I am coming Lord, coming now to Thee . . . *Salumanga aungnik makeruak angaroarani* . . . wash me, cleanse me in the blood that flows from Calvary."

Among them was a young Catholic couple, Bill and Annie Goose. This young couple later became the strongest Christian witness in that village. Their lives were totally changed by the power of God. Before this they had been involved in the dreadful drunken fights. Sometimes it had been necessary to bring in a plane to rush the injured off to the Yellowknife Hospital. But now this young couple was wonderfully transformed by the power of God.

Later on Bill's parents too committed their lives to Christ, and a great change took place. "Since I found the Lord I am not the same and I'll never be the same again," is a favorite chorus of our Eskimo Christians. A few months later the people of Holman Island gave us a building, inviting us to establish a mission there.

The cry of the unreached villages always rang in my ears. We must keep reaching out, taking the gospel to others. One spring we planned a long snowmobile trek to caribou camps, 400 miles across the barren lands and polar sea ice. We spent considerable time getting the equipment in order, the sleds lashed, the forty-five-gallon barrel of gas on the sled. We had to take all our gas supply with us for there was none available where we were going. Our guide had an old snowmobile, and as we left I actually wondered if it would ever complete the trip.

At first the traveling was very pleasant as the two snowmobiles bumped along over the snow. But soon we hit the rough sea ice and there we began the struggle of maneuvering the snowmobiles and sled over those tangled hunks of ice. Sometimes the sled would get snagged in the ice and we'd struggle to lift it out before we could proceed. Occasionally it would upset and we would again be delayed. Progress through the sea ice was very slow and difficult. We bounced and banged along over the hard drifts until it seemed every muscle in our bodies ached.

At the end of the long day of travel we set up camp. This meant wearily unloading the sled, struggling with cold hands to pitch the tent and digging through the two feet of snow on the lake to make a platform for sleeping. Last of all, we had to bring in the primus stove and frozen food.

"Titoitsi . . . come and have tea" was the call from one tent to another, and almost instantly the Eskimo guides responded, coming in for a cup of tea and supper. The little children fell asleep during the meal. In fact, we all felt so sleepy and tired from the first day of travel, that in no time we snuggled into bed. Stretching out on the snow platform with just a caribou skin and sleeping bag between us and the snow suddenly seemed delightful, because it was warm. We didn't even notice its hardness.

About six in the morning I crawled out of my sleeping bag, lit the primus stove which quickly heated the little tent, and melted ice for tea. Again we called *titoitsi* and everyone congregated in the little tent for breakfast, perhaps frozen fish or canned meat, and pilot biscuits. Then we hit the trail again for another day of hard travel.

I had taken Gwen along, and her three-year-old daughter who was a true Eskimo traveler. Through those long hours she sat bouncing on the sled. Even when the winds blew she never complained, never cried.

When it came time for the "mug up," it was also time for toilet routine and that little gal would have to go to the bathroom out in the open with the wind blowing, even in the minus-30 degree weather. No one went behind snow banks. This was just accepted as part of arctic travel.

Finally in the distance we saw the camp—not a village teeming with people, but just a little cluster of five or six tents and one igloo. This is what we had come these two days' travel to reach.

The people of this little village welcomed us very graciously and shared freely the little they had. After we enjoyed the usual cup of tea and lunch, we set up our own tent, and then went from tent to tent visiting with the people, endeavoring to witness to them. We stayed three days and then moved on to another camp. We visited three camps in all and then started the long journey back to Cambridge Bay. This 400-mile trek that would have taken three weeks by dog sled, took us about ten days, and was the longest trip I ever made by snowmobile.

CHAPTER 28

God Doesn't Forget

The desire to reach out to their own people was very deep in the hearts of Ron and Leonie Duffy. Leonie was a beautiful Eskimo girl from Coral Harbor, an island at the top of Hudson's Bay in the eastern Arctic. Her husband, Ron, a white man, had been raised in a boys' home in Montreal. The two had met in Churchill where Ron was a hostel supervisor and Leonie, a student. Later they were married and Ron's government job brought him to Cambridge Bay.

In Cambridge Bay, Ron and Leonie were both devout churchgoers. But something was missing in their lives. After a while they also became houseparents at the hostel and worked very closely with Nels and Ruth Pulk, the hostel supervisors. Ruth began to pray for Leonie, visiting her and telling her about Jesus. Leonie became interested and began searching. Finally one evening Leonie decided to come to our church.

One Friday night she came in and sat at the back. As I was preaching, God's Spirit was speaking to Leonie. She responded to

God's call and gave her all to Jesus that night. The wonderful experience of being "born again" was hers. Now she not only knew about the Lord; she knew Him personally.

A close bond developed between Leonie and me. She became very keen to learn God's way and God's Word. Lovingly, I called her *paniga* (my daughter), and she looked upon me as her spiritual mother. Leonie was the one who during her Bible reading came upon the scriptural teaching about water baptism. She wouldn't rest until we had a water baptismal service. And it was Leonie who had to come back for a second plunge deep in the water to be sure she had gone all the way with her Lord.

A tremendous desire began to burn in this young Christian's heart to reach her own people. Very soon she wrote to her friends and loved ones at Coral Harbor and told them of the wonderful experience of salvation that had come to her life.

The next week her husband Ron too surrendered his life to the Lord. Together they began their Christian walk. Of all our Bible school students, none had more zeal than Ron and Leonie.

When the Holy Ghost outpouring was at its height in Cambridge Bay, no one was at the altar more often and stayed longer than Leonie; yet she did not receive the baptism in the Spirit at that time.

Months later, one Sunday at about midnight, my phone rang. It was Leonie. "I want to come down and pray in the church. May I?"

I told her that she was welcome to do so, and in a few minutes I heard footsteps on the stairway. Akana had come with Leonie and it was a beautiful sound to hear these two earnestly praying in their own Eskimo tongue, worshiping and adoring the Lord Jesus Christ whom they loved.

I was on my way to bed but felt compelled to join them. About three in the morning the prayer meeting was still on. Leonie had moved into a depth of prayer. Obviously the Lord was visiting her. Akana and I just remained in prayer ourselves, trusting that the Lord would have His way and meet this deep desire in Leonie's heart to receive more from God.

About 3:30 kneeling all by herself in a corner of the prayer room, Leonie received this wonderful experience of being filled with the Holy Ghost as she burst out speaking a language she had never learned. Oh, the victory and joy it brought to her! She was being prepared to carry the message to her own people. A little later on, in the quietness of their home, Ron also received this same infilling of the Holy Spirit as the Christians gathered together for a time of fellowship.

After two years in Bible school, word came that Ron and Leonie were being transferred to Baker Lake, a large Eskimo village with over 800 people. Ron would be the settlement manager, so this was quite a promotion. It meant a good paying job, with a lovely split-level, fully modern house. Reluctantly I bade them farewell; yet I had to congratulate Ron and wish him God's best in his new responsibility. He had done well to climb to this government position.

A year later I had a phone call from Ron. Their last few summer holidays had been spent in Coral Harbor where they had witnessed to family and friends, and had seen several commit their lives to Christ. Now this young nucleus of Christians needed help. They had asked Ron and Leonie to come.

"So we're going, Kayy," they told me.

"But what about your good job, your lovely home? Where will you live?" I asked.

"We're trusting the Lord, Kayy. Come and see us as soon as you can."

All I could say was, "Bless you both, Ron and Leonie." I somehow knew God would see this couple through and teach them the ways of faith.

After talking with them, I hung up the phone, pulled on my parka, and jumped on my snowmobile. Up the hill I rode to keep an appointment with God, reminding Him of a promise made to me eighteen long years before.

In 1957 one cold winter morning I had climbed the hill just behind the village to Tuk, seeking inspiration and strength from above. As I stood on that little hill alone, the northeast wind was swirling the snow about my feet and blowing snow in my face; the trim around my parka hood was coated with frost and my lashes were so frosted I couldn't close my eyes.

It was my second year in the north and as I turned my face eastward, my mind suddenly thought of the many Eskimo villages across those barren lands, across that arctic coastline for 2,500 miles, that had not been visited by the Holy Ghost power of God.

A faith arose within me that was not my own. It came from above. The Scripture flashed into my mind of Caleb pleading with Joshua: "Give me this mountain" (Josh. 14:12 KJV). Standing there in the full flush of faith, with my hands extended toward God and my face toward the east, I prayed: "Oh, God, give us this arctic coastline. Let there be a witness of the gospel and power of God in every Eskimo village and settlement in my generation!"

Somehow I knew God had heard. And the Lord also revealed that the only possible way this could happen would be if we had our own aircraft. The distances to travel are so great; commercial aircraft fly so infrequently and are so expensive. The only way to get it all together would be with a mission aircraft. An expectation, a new confidence, was born in my heart that day while standing alone on the hill. God would one day give us an aircraft. I knew it. Oh, the joy that soared through my heart!

With swelling expectations, I slid down the hill back to my little house. In my youthful zeal I thought surely on the next mail plane there would be something about this aircraft, but there was nothing. Next week there was nothing, next month there was still nothing.

The years came and went. Ten years later I was still running behind dog teams trying to reach Eskimos for Jesus. Fifteen long years later, I was bouncing across those barren lands on snowmobile treks. And yet in my heart the vision burned. "For the vision is yet for an appointed time . . . though it tarry, wait for it; because it will surely come" (Hab. 2:3 KJV).

Telling no one what was in my heart, I decided I would know it was God's time to bring this to pass when He would cause those over me in the Lord to be in agreement. The years passed and I continued to wait.

Finally, in the summer of 1975, I brought up the airplane subject to my pastor, Maureen Gaglardi. Pastor Gaglardi considered that if I still felt it was God's will, she was in agreement.

"But, Kayy," she reminded, "you know the missionary society funds are strapped to the limit. You'll have to go out and raise the funds for the aircraft yourself." Again something leaped in my heart. I was sure it would only take me about two years to raise $60,000, the price of a suitable aircraft.

Two months after this, I was invited by Pastor John Lucas to Immanuel Assembly in Calgary, Canada. We needed missionaries for Holman Island and I had approached Pastor Lucas about the possibility of sending a young couple there. He had agreed and invited me to Calgary to help orientate the young couple for their future arctic life.

On Sunday, Pastor Lucas asked me, "Kayy, I want you to share your vision of the Arctic." I hesitated. His church was now accepting the added financial responsibility of totally supporting this young couple at Holman Island and I felt that was a big strain on their budget. But he pressed me, "Share your burden, Kayy, your vision for the Arctic."

For the first time I felt at liberty to speak freely about the need of an airplane, because now my pastor was in agreement. A principle of God's Word is that we submit to and obey those whom God puts over us in the Lord. That evening I presented some slides of the Arctic and then opened my heart about the need for an aircraft, telling them of my vision eighteen years earlier on the hill at Tuk; how that often during that time I'd go out and climb a hill, till the

Eskimos finally decided that Kayy just likes to climb hills. Little did they know that every time I climbed a hill, I again looked eastward and cried, "Oh, God, remember the promise you gave me on that hill in Tuk. I'm still waiting, Lord."

That Sunday night in Calgary, as I presented the need of the aircraft to reach every Eskimo village with the gospel of power, something was born in that congregation. Their hearts were knit together with the Arctic and the needs of the Eskimo people.

I finished my message and turned to sit down, but Pastor Lucas was insistent. "Talk some more about the airplane," he said. I returned to the pulpit and spoke for another ten minutes. Then he stood up and said, "We're going to take up an offering for that plane, right now."

Over $4,000 came in. Tremendous! I thought.

At the close of the service, a young man came striding up the aisle. "Kayy," he said, "if you get that aircraft and need a pilot, you've got one." Danny Perrault was a commercial pilot with engineer's papers, working as a flight instructor at the Calgary flying club. God had put it in his heart to be a missionary pilot and he was willing to go.

"What about your wife?" I asked.

"Just a minute," he said.

In seconds, Margie was at his side, and she was bubbling. "Praise the Lord! We've been praying for an opportunity to fly a plane for Jesus!" she said. It was a thrilling night, and more was to come.

I flew on to Toronto and on the third day, Pastor Lucas called me from Calgary. "I just want you to know the people are still giving. $12,000 is now in the kitty for the airplane!"

I was overwhelmed! A few days later another phone call came from John. "$62,000 is now available for the purchase of that arctic airplane!"

I could hardly believe my ears. $62,000! What I had waited

eighteen years for, in God's time He gave to us in just *ten* days. As I hung up the receiver, tears of gratitude were flowing down my cheeks. "God, you didn't forget. You remembered all the time. Eighteen long years!"

"Just hang in there, Kayy," Pastor Lucas said. "We'll have you airborne in six months!"

CHAPTER 29

More Opportunities

Following my trip to Toronto I had another phone call from Ron Duffy in Coral Harbor. "Kayy," he asked, "can you come for some meetings? The people want a baptismal service and they need the Holy Ghost experience. Come and teach us more of God's Word." What a joy it was for me to answer this call.

In the fall of 1975 I flew by commercial airline to Coral Harbor, pushing farther into the east than I had previously been. I was amazed at the work Ron and Leonie had accomplished in ten short months.

Faithfully they had preached the gospel and taught the people. Ron was a real motivator; he delighted in helping the Eskimos help themselves. And now as he entered church work full time, his main objective was to motivate the people and teach them so they could carry on their own work for God. Two old buildings were given to them and with the help of the Christian Eskimos, they transformed these buildings into a comfortable little chapel. They taught the Christians to tithe, so from the very beginning this little work was entirely self-supporting.

A group of Christians was established in the church with a fine Sunday school and obviously Ron and Leonie were recognized as spiritual leaders. People came with problems, often phoning Leonie for counsel, asking questions about the Scriptures. It had all the earmarks of a healthy work.

During that first visit to Coral Harbor, we had a great water baptismal service with Eskimos coming in from as far away as Rankin Inlet and Eskimo Point. They, too, wanted to receive more teaching and understanding from God's Word. What an awakening there was in the land! Truly God was accelerating His work. Obviously it was God's time for this eastern Arctic area. In less than a year a new church had burst into life and the people had been led on and established in God. Some received the Holy Spirit experience while I was there; others were still seeking, and I knew God would continue to move and fill many with the Holy Ghost and power.

While in Coral Harbor, I had a phone call from Rankin Inlet. The leader of another new Christian group, David Arglukark, was asking if I could come over for some meetings before I went south. A Christian group in Rankin Inlet too? "Praise the Lord! I'll be there."

How had God's fire started in Rankin? I wondered as we flew over from Coral. High up on the western shore of Hudson's Bay, Rankin was a large settlement of 800 Eskimos and a few hundred white people, with a reputation for being rough and tough, with a tremendous drinking problem. I knew there were a few, truly committed Christians living there.

In August, 1975 (this was now November), David and Dorothy Arglukark, a young Eskimo Christian couple, had moved to Rankin Inlet from Eskimo Point. Dorothy, a most attractive Eskimo woman, was born and raised in an igloo, and it wasn't until she was thirteen or fourteen years of age that she had much contact with white people.

They had moved to the village of Rankin Inlet where her father was to work in a mine, and there she attended school for about one year. When she was sixteen, Dorothy married David and they moved to Eskimo Point where they came to know the Lord through Rev. Armand Tagoona, an outstanding Eskimo preacher.

"Then John Maksagak came along and taught us the deeper truths of God," they told me. John Maksagak! As I had traveled through the settlements of the eastern Arctic, I was thrilled to discover the work John had been doing. God had blessed John with a new appointment as chairman of the cultural institute. As such, he traveled with a group of Eskimo people from various settlements to locations all across the north for conferences and discussions.

After the business of the day, John held meetings in the homes where he was asked many questions about his faith. Although he had never boasted or even spoken of his accomplishments, I found that a number had been saved and many helped through his able ministry.

Traveling with John often was one of the young men from the church in Tuk, Randy Polkiak, who also had been appointed to the cultural institute. Together they had the opportunity to share their Christian witness in many communities.

One official trip took them to Eskimo Point. Dorothy and David had moved back to Rankin Inlet, but they, too, traveled to Eskimo Point to attend the meetings. In those evening gatherings, Dorothy was deeply impressed by John's testimony of the power of the Holy Spirit in his life, and this sparked the desire in her heart for more from God.

As she returned to Rankin Inlet, the desire grew, but no one in that community could help her. As best she could with her limited English, Dorothy searched God's Word. She wrote away for books on the Holy Spirit.

Dorothy told me that on August 15, 1975, as she knelt for prayer in her little kitchen, she tearfully besought the Lord to grant her the baptism in the Spirit she'd read about in the Bible. God, who responds to the earnest desires and longings of His children, came down and met this young Eskimo woman, all alone seeking Him. And there He wonderfully baptized her with His Holy Spirit. A new language she had never learned burst from her lips as a heavenly joy filled her being.

A remarkable change took place in Dorothy and she began to tell everyone the difference the Holy Ghost makes. New strength and power and joy was hers in Christ. As she shared this witness with everyone she came in contact with, God began to move in that little village. The few Christians who were there became hungry for more from God, and they, too, were filled with the Holy Ghost.

At first her husband was quite upset that Dorothy had received the Holy Ghost and he hadn't. But before long God met David and he, too, was baptized in the Holy Ghost. This kindled a fire in that village and soon it reached out, saving many from lives of drunkenness and sin. It spread and spread. When I reached Rankin Inlet in late November of the same year, I was amazed to find thirty to forty Christians, many of them brand new believers, wonderfully saved, and many of them already filled with the Holy Ghost.

Dorothy's husband, David Arglukark, is now the pastor at Rankin and he has been elected by his people as president of the Keewatin Inuit association. This means David must travel into some eight different communities in his job, also giving him many contacts for the Lord Jesus Christ.

While I was still in Rankin Inlet I received news that two men were on their way from Eskimo Point, about twelve hours hard snowmobile travel. They had some important things to discuss with me before I left.

One of these men turned out to be Tagak Curley, a colorful, highly intelligent Eskimo in his late thirties. Tagak is the recognized leader of the Eskimo in all of the Canadian Arctic, a man who has done much for the betterment of his people. Fluent in both English and Eskimo and possessing great organizational abilities, he was chosen to form and head up the Inuit Tapisariat—the Eskimo brotherhood—a strong, government-sponsored organization dedicated to the well-being of the Eskimo people.

Tagak had just become a Christian three years before. Now his great concern was how to reach his people with the gospel of Jesus Christ and the Holy Ghost message. He talked to me about the need of the Christians being of one heart and one mind in the Arctic.

As he had learned in the organizational structure in the government, it wasn't enough just to say we would be one; he felt we needed to bind together in one organization. And this was his main reason for coming to see me: they wanted to be a part of the Glad Tidings Missionary Society in the Arctic. His desire was to see a strong work established in Eskimo Point as well as in many other villages.

Because of Tagak's great ability he was appointed the executive director for the cultural institute, based in Eskimo Point. It was a delight to visit his very modern executive office, to see the carefully mapped out program, with eight or ten smaller offices manned by Eskimo personnel working in many aspects to maintain Eskimo culture in the north.

Tagak's influential position carries him to many parts of the Arctic, and as he does his job to the best of his ability, he also has many opportunities to witness for Jesus Christ.

With Tagak was another strong Eskimo leader, Charlie Inuarak, the representative from Pond Inlet to the Inuit Cultural Institute. Charlie was an outgoing Eskimo, with definite opinions, and most verbal about them. Just a few months previous to this he, too, had experienced a deeper walk with the Lord. Charlie had been interested in the truth of the Holy Ghost message, and while ministering to his own Eskimo people in Pangnirtung, again the fire burned and Charlie received this blessing from God. Back in his home in Pond Inlet, his wife too was wonderfully filled with the Holy Spirit.

Later Charlie was appointed by his people to the Eskimo brotherhood's orthography committee which was studying the possibility of combining the many Eskimo dialects into a common written language. He did his government work faithfully and then instead of wasting his evening hours in idle chatter, he would use the community hall or an Eskimo home for gospel meetings, spending all his off hours talking to his people about spiritual matters. God has blessed him and he has been instrumental in winning many of his own people to Christ.

Now he has a great desire to go full time into the Lord's service, and very shortly this flaming Eskimo evangelist will be accompanying us on the aircraft to some of the villages that he has visited, as well as new ones.

In November, 1975, Immanuel Assembly purchased a brand-new, five-seater Cessna 185. The very best of radio equipment was to be installed, as well as extra fuel storage "tip tanks" for long distance flying. The plane was quickly readied for the tough job of arctic flying that lay ahead.

Danny Perrault was accepted as the pilot and he and his wife immediately began plans for disposing of their home and moving into the Arctic. We would base the plane at Cambridge Bay. An empty house on the mission compound would be home for Danny's family. From that base we would work out to the other settlements. It was exciting!

Just four months later on March 15, 1976, the little Cessna landed in Cambridge Bay. At Danny's side in the co-pilot seat was Don Violette, the veteran arctic missionary. What could be a better combination to launch this new thrust answering the cry of the unreached areas beyond the Arctic Circle?

A few days after Danny had successfully flown the plane in, his wife and three children arrived in Cambridge Bay on the commercial airline. And on March 20, I flew in to launch the airplane ministry for Jesus Christ.

On March 22, we were planning our first trip to Holman Island where Frank and Liz Amantea, missionaries from Immanuel Assembly in Calgary, were pastoring. Our first gospel team included Doris Kekpak, the outstanding witness for Jesus who had been with me when we first visited Holman. The people loved her and were very responsive to her. It seemed fitting that she should be on this first trip with the new missionary airplane.

However, true to northern form, the weather was out. The wind was blowing and visibility was very poor, so we had to wait another day. The next morning Danny decided the weather was suitable for flying. The wind again began to pick up as the men prepared the aircraft for departure. It was cold—35 to 40 degrees below. The old mission truck creaked and groaned its protest as it struggled to pull the plane out of the snowdrift. And then we were all belted in, ready to go. But before taking off, Danny said, "Let's pray." So he committed the trip to the Lord. This has become the pattern for all flights.

It was a difficult flight. There was no beacon at Holman, so we were flying by instruments and aerial maps. Yet, two-and-one-half hours later we were directly on course. Beneath us the little settlement came into view.

What a thrill it was! I could only praise, "Oh, God, great is thy faithfulness!" As I looked down on the rough ice and snow formations below us, my mind went back to the days spent running behind the dog teams, cold, tired and sometimes lost.

My mind flashed back to those long hours and days of tedious snowmobile travel. I could almost feel the cold and numbness that would come into my hands, those aching muscles and tired bones from jolting across washboard drifts and jagged ice. As I sat comfortably in the little Cessna 185, a deep sense of gratitude welled up within me, "To God be the glory!"

There was great excitement as the new plane circled Holman and then touched down on the gravel airstrip located in the center of the settlement, now well covered by snow and ice. Before we could get out of the plane, Bill Goose, our first convert at Holman, had taken his hand from his big fur mitten. "Praise the Lord!" he exulted with excitement dancing from him. "It's here. The plane is really here!" There were strong handshakes all around, but most of all the Christians wanted to shake hands with Danny, the pilot of their wonderful new plane.

After two days of visiting and meetings, we moved on. Flying again by instruments, we headed farther north and west to the settlement of Sachs Harbor on the shores of Banks Island. Vancouverites, Bill and Ethel Goward, had just moved to establish a new church at the request of a small nucleus of Eskimo Christians.

Our next stop was Tuk and as we circled the village I caught sight of the little hill where I had stood and cried out to God to give us the Arctic for Christ. This Cessna 185 was His answer.

There was great excitement in Tuk that day as they rejoiced over the plane. And then they proudly showed us their fine, new, two-story church with a four-bedroom apartment upstairs that had been built during Dave and Velma Freeman's ministry there.

Back in Cambridge Bay, William Apsimik and Frank Analok were preparing eagerly for our first big thrust into the eastern Arctic. One week before Easter, 1976, we took off amid low, blowing snow—William, Frank, Danny and myself. Danny climbed to 10,000 feet for the 460-mile, non-stop flight over unfamiliar territory. As we came down through the clouds flying over the rough ice mass of Hudson's Bay en route to Coral Harbor, I remembered the vision God permitted me to actually see four years earlier, the only real vision of my life.

It was at midnight in Pastor Heubert's church in Chilliwack, B.C. I was praying fervently for the northland, remembering those many Eskimo villages that were unreached with the gospel of power. All at once, before my eyes I literally saw that land of ice and snow, that rugged arctic coastline that I knew so well. And then I saw a fire beginning to burn in the ice in one corner. It was such a strange sight. I smiled and said, "Can fire burn in ice?"

I felt the Spirit of the Lord speak to me and say, "Yes, and indeed a fire shall burn in the land of ice and snow, a fire of the Holy Ghost." That little fire suddenly began to spread and spread until it had crossed all that coast of ice and snow. "And so shall the fire of my Spirit burn across the northland. It will move in every village and every settlement. It will spread like wildfire. The fire will melt the icy hearts and change the face of the Arctic." And then the vision was gone. The fire was indeed kindled—praise God—and this was just the beginning.

Flying to Coral Harbor, a warm air front had moved in causing a build-up of ice on the wing tips and propeller. Danny changed his altitude but the ice hung on.

"Kayy, I don't like this wing ice," he quietly confided. There was nothing to do but pray for a good landing at Coral Harbor. Danny is so very safety conscious, and there is a sureness about his manner that makes his passengers feel totally secure when he is at the controls. Not only is he a fine pilot, but we know that even when we are beyond radio contact on these long range flights, there is never a time when Danny is out of touch with the main control tower that is based in heaven.

"We should be over Coral in eight minutes," Danny predicted, checking his aerial maps. I glanced at my watch. Sure enough, exactly eight minutes later we were buzzing the village. The winds were high and swirling snow obscured the strip as we touched down, but it was a good landing.

We had radioed ahead our expected arrival time, and every Christian family was there to greet us. For eight miles they had bumped across the drifts in cold, blowy weather.

Their thrill to see the new aircraft was beyond words. Each one touched and stroked the plane lovingly. They all had to clamber up for a look at the cockpit. "Praise the Lord!—our mission plane!" they exclaimed among themselves, laughing, shaking the hand of the *tingmisokti* (the pilot).

The men happily helped Danny tie the plane down to the fuel oil drums, pull the insulated cover over the engine, and then in high spirits, they bore us off in a bombardier for the hour's ride to town.

The Christians were especially delighted to meet our gospel team members, and gave Frank and William a warm welcome. Each night the church was packed. Frank and William taught new gospel songs, exhorted and testified. The lively singing, mostly in Eskimo, blessed many hearts. Several responded to the gospel. Leo, a young man in his early twenties, later testified, "I had been on drugs, but Jesus Christ has set me completely free!"

For seven days we held a Bible teaching seminar for the Eskimo Christians, with Danny running a shuttle service to Rankin Inlet, Whale Cove and Eskimo Point, bringing in the church leaders of those communities. Pastor and Mrs. Heubert from British Columbia arrived on the weekly commercial flight to join our teaching team.

These Eskimo men and women devoured God's Word with an eagerness I had never seen before. During those daily afternoon and evening sessions, their hunger and fresh desire pulled the teaching from us, so anxious are they to equip themselves to reach others.

While we were in Coral, the worst storm of the winter blew in, with heavy snow and gale winds. Would the tie-downs hold the plane? Would the snowdrifts damage the wings? With visibility zero there was no movement in the village, no way we could check it out. "Please, dear God, look after our plane," the Eskimos fervently prayed.

When Danny was finally able to get out to the plane, he scrambled up over fourteen-foot drifts and there was the plane, unharmed by the storm that had raged around it.

With another gospel team of four fired-up Eskimo Christians from Coral Harbor, we set out to visit Rankin Inlet, Eskimo Point and Whale Cove. The distances were close enough to shuttle them in. These Eskimo teams were a tremendous blessing everywhere we went—Eskimos reaching Eskimos for God. There was a real response to their ministry of singing and preaching. Souls were saved, several filled with the Holy Spirit and many believers inspired and encouraged to press on.

In Rankin Inlet it was my privilege to dedicate their new church to the glory of God. They had transformed an old workshop into a comfortable chapel, complete with handsome plywood pews. In less than eight months, this Christian group had come into being and was totally self-supporting. There were now fifty to sixty people keenly involved, and the burning desire of their hearts was to spread the fire to others.

Everywhere they rejoiced to see the plane, passing around the hat in every community towards the expense of operating the aircraft. Not only are they enjoying the blessing of what God is doing, but they are also willing to assume responsibility. "We want to help keep that plane flying, Kayy. We want you to take Eskimo gospel teams into every village and settlement across the north. We want our brothers to hear the simple gospel message, to experience the Holy Ghost power that has changed our lives."

CHAPTER 30

Treasures of the Snow

After these two exhilarating months of crisscrossing the Arctic, it was time to fly south to rehearse in the ears of the Calgary church the wonderful things God has done and is doing through the new aircraft they have so generously supplied.

The weather was out that Saturday in May, 1976, as we awakened. Danny checked all morning but it only worsened. The ceiling was very low. There was no hope of movement that day. Again he checked in the afternoon. There was a slight improvement.

"If we want to connect with that flight to Winnipeg, let's go, Kayy," he said. "It'll take a full hour and forty-five minutes. All being well, we might even give you fifteen minutes to change planes!"

Quickly we went out to the airstrip and piled into the plane. Danny checked it out and soon we were in the air, flying through snow and thick, low-lying clouds with only occasional glimpses of land below or sky above. In these ice fogs and white-outs you are never certain of how close you are to the ground.

Dropping out of a cloud we caught sight of the strip. Thankfully, we sat down and taxied to the tower. From Churchill I was to catch a commercial flight south.

As I transferred to another airplane, Danny rolled down the runway, revved up and took off. And then with a farewell dip of a wing he was off, back to the Arctic, to the thirty-two Eskimo settlements that are waiting for the Word of God to be preached in all its fullness. The Spirit is working among the Eskimos in a mighty way during these last days. He is bringing them not only from the darkness of Stone Age heathenism, but also from the awful sins of modern "civilization," transforming them into vibrant witnesses for the power of Jesus Christ.

I thought of the old Eskimo sitting in Charlie's tiny shack at Reindeer Station all those years ago . . . a small, stooped, wizened man who had weathered many a blizzard, and with deep searching eyes he had turned to me. "Kayy, how long have you known about this Jesus?"

"All my life," I said.

"And did your parents know?" he probed.

"Yes."

"And your grandparents?"

"Yes," I answered.

"Then why has it taken you white people so long to tell us Eskimos about Christ?"

And it was with this burden weighing on my heart that I had climbed the hill at Tuk and cried to God: "Oh, God, give us every Eskimo village." Praise God, He is doing it!

I remembered that mid-January as Florence and I had looked out at the first red glow in the dark of winter with its promise of sunrise and light—and God spoke to my heart reassuring me that His light would be spread abroad in the Arctic.

Praise God! In this land of the long winter night, the light of the glorious gospel of Jesus Christ is shining in many hearts. God willing, by 1978 it will be shining in every village of Eskimo land. God's Holy Spirit is rescuing His precious Eskimo people from a life of bleak hopelessness to a fullness of joy they never imagined. They are "gifts to God that he delights in" (Eph. 1:11 TLB)—truly "treasures of the snow" (Job 38:22 KJV).

I remembered the vision that God had given to me in that little church in Chilliwack of a small fire off in a corner suddenly blazing, then racing, sweeping across the vast arctic wilderness of ice and snow, a fire in ice crossing the whole northland. "Can fire burn in ice?" I had asked. Praise God, it can.

The fire of His Holy Spirit is quickening and strengthening and emboldening the Eskimo people, filling their lives with miracles of faith and joy so that in God's power and might they are carrying the fire from settlement to settlement—God's Holy Ghost fire that has indeed melted icy hearts and is changing the face of the Arctic.

With the aircraft, with these fiery gospel teams, God has given us the tools to finish the work. We dare not lay them down, we will not rest, until the fire of God is blazing brightly in every Eskimo settlement across the north—God's fire on ice.

May 20, 1977

Epilogue

On October 17, 1976, with Florence Erickson, I once again headed north. During these past seven months we have crisscrossed the Arctic, from Alaska to the east coast of Baffin Island, logging some 40,000 miles and 300 hours of air time. The gas bill alone was $8,000. We visited twenty-one communities; for six of them, this was the first time they had heard the gospel of Holy Ghost power preached fully and simply.

For thousands of miles we flew over desolate, barren, uninhabited land, with only an occasional glimpse of a small herd of caribou or musk oxen roaming below. For many long hours we flew over the treacherous, broken ice of the Arctic Ocean; one plunge into those chilling waters and the game would be over for us all. The awareness of deadly hazards below, and flights through unpredictable changes of wind and weather have quickened our prayers that God would some day give us a twin-engine aircraft for safety sake.

To begin the tour, with Danny I flew east to Rankin Inlet, holding our first five-day seminar there. All the Christians eagerly attended. From there we moved on, taking with us Eskimo Christians to sing and exhort their fellow natives to "Repent, and be baptized every one of you in the name of Jesus Christ for the remission of sins, and ye shall receive the gift of the Holy Ghost" (Acts 2:38 KJV). I was amazed to see how these young believers had grown in God. Night after night the altars were lined with humble Eskimos seeking salvation and the infilling of the Holy Spirit.

In Cape Dorset after the first service, thirty to forty young people stayed behind to ask more questions about this Jesus. In Spence Bay, at least another thirty people crowded into the house where we stayed to sing and discuss God's Word for hours. Can you imagine the thrill of seeing that crowd of young people kneel and sing prayerfully, "Come into my heart, Lord Jesus!"

In another remote village on Baffin Island, I thought we were back in the Book of Acts. The people never seemed to tire of long services, beginning at 9 P.M. and continuing until three or four in the morning. (Good thing there were no high windows to fall out of!)

When we returned four months later to that village, towards the end of this tour, there was an unusual outpouring of the Holy Spirit, such as I had not witnessed before. It was much like the house meeting in Acts 10. I had preached, and then Dorothy Arglukark led the people in prayer and praise, encouraging them to receive from God. Suddenly, just like in Cornelius's house, the Holy Ghost "fell." At the same instant, the people all began to speak in tongues, having received the power and joy of God's Holy Spirit.

Only one Christian woman did not share in this wonder. She spent the entire following day in prayer and reading God's Word. About supper time she asked Dorothy to join her.

"Why did I not receive the Holy Ghost too?" she pled. Again Dorothy encouraged her to believe, and in the quietness of her own bedroom, God's Holy Spirit came down, filling this dear Eskimo woman with heavenly language and great joy. Later that same evening, in the home next door, another team member, Louie Bruce, had the joy of leading his host's wife to the Lord. Wherever we went, Louie spent whole nights patiently explaining God's Word to hungry Eskimos.

In Spence Bay, we sat down in the brilliant morning sunlight on the bay ice where a strip had been cleared, and were warmly welcomed by Eskimos. We secured the use of the adult education building for the evening service in this village of some 500 residents. But how many would come? A big wedding was also scheduled for that night at the Roman Catholic church.

"There are nineteen snowmobiles parked outside the church," we were told.

But at 8 P.M. what a sight it was to see snowmobiles zooming in from all over the village; people were seen running from the wedding to our service. In fact, the wedding dance was delayed till after our service! Soon the building was jam-packed with at least 250 Eskimos, anxious to hear about the "gospel of power."

Night after night they came. Soon, throughout the village, the children and young people were singing our theme song, "God loves you and I love you and that's the way it's going to be." In this community on the shores of the Arctic Ocean, the people are so open-hearted towards the gospel message, and so very anxious to learn.

At Baker Lake, among those who sought the Lord was a young Eskimo woman whose search for peace had taken her as far as 1200 miles south to Winnipeg in vain. One night during our little house meeting she surrendered her life to Christ and was filled with true peace and joy.

In Holman Island twenty-four people followed the Lord in the waters of baptism. We carried with us on the plane Holman's portable water baptismal tank—seven feet long, two feet wide and three feet deep, made of canvas with a plastic liner all supported with two-inch plastic tubing.

In Sachs Harbor, we set it up in the living room (which also serves as a chapel) of the missionary's home for their first water baptismal service. Seven believers were baptized. In the churches at Tuktoyaktuk and Cambridge Bay, we baptized another fourteen. It was such a blessing for them that many asked, "Can I get baptized again?" In Tuktoyaktuk, I married a couple on Saturday night and baptized them on Sunday night.

What a joy it is to see our natives increasingly taking leadership roles to carry on the ministry! Last September, before I arrived back in the north, John Maksagak conducted their first baptismal service in Rankin Inlet, baptizing eighteen converts. He also performed a wedding ceremony during that visit. (John is also a justice of the peace.)

We have just completed a ten-day leaders' conference in Cambridge Bay, with eighteen workers flown in from western, central and eastern Arctic. (All but five of these were Eskimos.)

Each day they sat through five to six hours of solid Bible teaching, never missing a class. Our teachers, Pastor David Kitely from Oakland, California, and Dorothy Williams, principal of Glad Tidings Bible College in Vancouver, marveled at the enthusiasm, the eagerness to learn that mark these Eskimo leaders. The questions they asked revealed a searching for the deep truths of God. And, as they spent a whole day in prayer together, crying to God, it was evident that God has burdened them for the souls of their fellow Eskimos.

Can we ease up now? No. We cannot and will not slacken our pace until the torch of leadership is firmly gripped by Eskimo hands to carry the message and keep the fires of Holy Ghost revival brightly blazing across the Arctic.

For further information about the work of arctic missions or to correspond with Kayy Gordon, you may write to:

> Glad Tidings Missionary Society
> 3456 Fraser Street
> Vancouver, B.C., V5V-4C4
> Canada